I've Been Shot At,
What's Your Excuse?

by Sherry Lawson

Sherry L Lawson

Lessons from my Life

I've Been Shot At! What's your Excuse?
Lessons from My Life

Copyright© 2007 by Sherry Lawson

All rights reserved. No part of this book may be used
or reproduced by any means; graphic, electronic or
mechanical, including photocopying, recording, taping or by
any information storage-retrieval system without the written
permission of the publisher, except in the case of brief
quotations embodied in critical articles and reviews.

This book may be ordered by contacting the author by:

mail:
P.O. Box 45
Longford Mills, Ontario L0K 1L0 or

e-mail:
maangdodem@hotmail.com

The views and memories expressed in this work
are solely those of the author.
Copy editing by Alice de Munnik
Cover and Book Design by Christine Bothman

ISBN: 978-0-9784980-0-9 (pbk)

Printed in Orillia, Ontario, Canada.

In library talk, this page is called a verso.

*To Granny Douglas (Nookomis)
who loved me so.*

"Out of suffering have emerged the strongest souls; the most massive characters are seared with scars."

Kahlil Gibran
Lebanese artist and poet in United States
1883-1931

Table of Contents

TITLE	PAGES
Fore-Word	1-3
My Father the Entrepreneur (September 2007)	4-7
The Question (April 2005)	8-10
Weather (April 2006)	11-15
To My Yet-Unborn Grandson (December 2004)	16-17
Uncle Terry (March 2006)	18-23
Three Months (January 2006)	24-26
Old George (March 2007)	27-31
Stop at the Mall (January 2005)	32-33
I've Been Shot At! What's Your Excuse? (September 2007)	34-36
My Public Library (Spring 2007)	37-39
Granny's Pitcher (March 2006)	40-42
Just Like My Childhood (October 1991)	43-45
Lake St. John (June 2005)	46-50
The Winter of 1981 (February 2007)	51-55
My Trip to Town (December 2006)	56-59
Firewood (February 2005)	60-62
Alberta Bound (October 2006)	63-66
Band Council Meeting in the Old Hall (December 2006)	67-70

School Pictures (October 2005) 71-75

From Wartime to School Time (June 2007) 76-79

Hands (April 2006) 80-83

The Lost Key (January 2007) 84-89

Almost Famous (September 2007) 90-95

After-Word 96

"Humus O Perdo"
left to right: Deborah Wagner, Ellen Cohen, Leila Sherriff, Sherry Lawson (April 2007).

Foreword

Two women who never met each other challenged me recently.

Donna Messer (donnamesser.com) is an author, speaker and trainer, who I met at a conference several years ago. Although I have spent very little time with her, Donna has deeply affected my life. She pushed me to figure out the time I am most alive. That was an easy answer to come up with. "When I'm telling stories about my life."

Donna told me "Then, do it! Take those very important stories and share them with the world. You need to do this. The world needs to hear you."

Donna was very direct: "How can I help you?"

She already had.

I have an older dear friend named Hilda. Now in her 80s, Hilda was widowed at an early age and trained as a nurse. She raised her boys on her own. She is a language keeper, a lady and my sounding board. It turns out she was also good friends with my beloved Granny.

Hilda, in her eternally soft, yet clear way, asked me how the writing of my life story was coming along.

"You know, slow", I answered. "I'm busy, you know."

Hilda patted my hand. "We're all busy, dear. So, do you think it will take you a lifetime to write down your stories?"

"Probably", I answered. "Every time I finish one, another pops into my head."

"Mmmm-hmmm", Hilda replied. "I see. So you think when you finish that last story, you'll be done? You'll never have to tell another story or write another one? You'll be very old, you know."

I laughed. "Yeah, I guess so."

Hilda continued. "Mmmm-hmmm. I see you as an old lady, sitting in your rocking chair, still using your hands, telling stories. And there are children at your feet and grandchildren. Oh, and I see moms and dads and grandparents sitting off to the side, listening carefully. Don't wait until then, dear. Don't wait until you have a book this thick." Hilda spread her thumb and forefinger apart as far as they could go.

"The world needs your stories now. They deserve your stories today. Don't make them wait."

Thanks, Hilda.

My dear friend, Brenda, continues to ask: "Is there a story in that book about me?" Since my famousness makes her so crazy, yes, Brenda is in this book. She is my buddy, attitude adjustment and cheerleader all in one. Brenda, I am sure, will make me sign her copy.

My husband, Robert, is a source of constant strength for me. Sure, he makes me run the numbers. But, at the end of it all, he wants me to do what makes me happy. A man of few words, he said, as I began to write, "What are you waiting for? You've always wanted to write a book." Our relationship has been described very aptly by our friend, Kelly. "Sherry, you are Rob's favourite movie."

A big chi-miigwech to my brother, Mark Douglas (Biidaunquad). For me, it's where the storytelling began.

My Lifescapes Alumni Group continues to meet monthly. Every member, especially Alice de Munnik, has encouraged me to continue. We all have laughed and cried together. Each one of them continues as my fan club. I am grateful for that.

Jayne Turvey, in charge of adult programming at the Orillia Public Library, welcomed me into the first Lifescapes Program over two years ago. I thought at the time that I didn't belong in a memoir-writing program! I was too young. I had nothing to write about. Jayne convinced me otherwise. I am eternally thankful for that. Thanks, Jayne.

As a charter member of "Humus o Perdo", I have been constantly reminded by my fellow members/friends to get busy and get my book published. Ellen Cohen, Leila Sherriff, Deborah Wagner, thank you for all you are to me. You continue to be a reliable bright spot in my life.

The sources of my stories are my family, my friends and, sometimes, even strangers. I hope you will come to know a small part of me and my world as I offer you this little peek into my life. In our tradition, our stories are not written down. Our tales are meant to be told face to face, passed down from father to son, grandmother to daughter. In this modern high-tech world, I'm compelled to break with Anishnaabe tradition and leave behind a written record.

These stories are not mine. I am only the teller. I am meant to give them away. I leave them here for my friends, my family, my children and my children's children.

Perhaps they will trigger a memory from your own experiences. I will have been successful if I have made you laugh or cry or, maybe, just leave a mundane world behind for three to seven minutes at a time.

Thank you (miigwech) for joining me on my journey.

Sherry Lawson
August 2007

My Father the Entrepreneur

My brother, Mark, the oldest, is the true storyteller in the family. He can spin a tale that always makes the listener think by connecting the dots.

To pay homage to my wiser, older sibling and with his permission, I share with you the following, one of Mark's favourites. It has a true local Orillia flavour and is an accurate reflection of the barriers faced by Native people.

*   *   *   *   *

My father, Irvin Jack Douglas, wasn't always a chief. When he was younger, he was a student and, much later, a veteran of the Second World War.

This story took place in the early 50s, a time when Native people, or Indians as we were called back then, were not even allowed to vote in federal elections. Indians could not consume or possess alcohol either until the 1960s.

My father was somewhat ahead of his time since he was a graduate of Shaw's Business College in Toronto. He must have been a star student. He had no problem writing letters in perfect form, drafting a proposal to Indian Affairs or performing simple bookkeeping. He was an excellent typist. This took place during those years when very few people on reserves had regular jobs. Times were tough and children often went hungry. My father wanted to find a way to perform more than poor-paying seasonal work.

My father considered community needs, gaps in service and his abilities as a businessman when he thought about starting a business. He had noticed a sign in the window of the Orillia branch of the Canadian Imperial Bank of Commerce that read: "We're here for the small business man." My father created a beautiful business plan, including projections of capital needs, depreciation, operating expenses (including office supplies) and full-time equivalent staff over a three-year period.

He made an appointment with the manager of the main street bank, since, in those days, only the manager could authorize loans. He dressed in his best suit, shined his shoes and practised his greeting in a mirror before heading to this important meeting.

After being ushered kindly into the branch by the manager, he was offered a seat in a private office. My father explained that he was applying for a loan to start a small business, a taxi company, at R.R. #6 Orillia. His plan was to buy a 1957 Plymouth, the first in a fleet of several he hoped to have.

The bank manager was suitably impressed with my father's very complete business plan. His proposed expenses were in line with what his somewhat limited market research would allow. He had saved half the amount necessary to buy a new car. He only needed to borrow the other half.

"Mr. Douglas", the bank manager said. "This is an extremely well done business plan – 30 pages. I daresay it is the best business plan I've seen for a long time."

My father's chest puffed with up pride. "Thank you, sir."

The bank manager continued. "Do I understand you correctly that your proposed business will be at R.R. #6 Orillia?"

"Yes sir!" My father was pleased with the way the meeting seemed to be going.

"I'm sorry, Mr. Douglas, but such a venture would be too risky for this bank. I cannot authorize a small business loan for you. However, if you were able to come up with a co-signer from the local community, a person of prominence, then I will reconsider your application."

My father was deflated, but polite, as he left the bank manager's office. He had a plan. He knew just who to ask to be his co-signer. But, it would take some real negotiations, considerable give and take and some time for the person to agree.

Wilbur Cramp was a member of a long-standing Orillia family, an entrepreneur himself, who had owned various pieces of real estate in the Orillia area. He had a little business at the end of Mississauga Street closest to the Carnegie Library. As a further tribute to his personal respectability, Mr. Cramp also carried keys to the liquor store located on the same block.

Apparently, on occasion, Wilbur Cramp would find himself in a situation where he might have to "borrow" a bottle of alcohol (or two) from said liquor store. Mr. Cramp was brutally honest and if a "loan" of alcohol was required, he always left a properly executed I.O.U. on the cash register. And he always paid what was owed as soon as the store was open again.

My father met Wilbur Cramp, as was their custom for more than a decade, in the back of his seed store after closing. It was a Friday afternoon. The negotiations went on for many hours, long into the night and even continued on into Saturday morning. At least once, the keys to the liquor store were brought out, and an I.O.U. was left on the cash register, dutifully signed by Mr. Cramp.

By Sunday morning, my father had what he needed, a signed letter of recommendation from his friend, the local businessman. A person of prominence agreed in writing to co-sign a small business loan for Irvin J. Douglas.

After taking it easy at home all of Sunday, my father got himself prepared to see the bank manager again, hopefully, the next day.

My father was so proud to be one step closer to his dream of owning a small business. He even had decided on the name. He had gotten prices for printing up business cards emblazoned with "Doug's Taxi Service."

The bank manager seemed surprised that my father had returned. My father explained how he had done exactly as the bank manager had asked. He had been successful in gaining the support of an Orillian of prominence. Mr. Wilbur Cramp had agreed to be his co-signer. My father, with a flourish, passed the letter across the large oak desk to the bank manager.

The bank manager seemed incredulous. "Mr. Douglas, it looks like this is His Worship's signature, Mayor Wib Cramp. Is that right?"

He came around the desk to show it to my father, who puffed up his chest again. "Yes, sir, that is the mayor's signature."

The bank manager repeated, "This is the signature of His Worship, Wilbur Cramp?"

My father responded, happy now that he had nothing to worry about. "Yes sir, that is a document signed by His Worship, Mayor Cramp, a person of prominence as you had requested."

The bank manager sat down heavily in his chair on the other side of the desk. He rested his forehead on his left hand. He shrugged and threw both of his hands in the air. "I'm very sorry, Mr. Douglas, to have to tell you this. In light of this unexpected turn of events, the bank will now require two co-signers."

As told by Mark Douglas (Biidaanakwad - "Cloud Approaching")

Mark Douglas (Biidaanakwad - "Cloud Approaching"), Sherry's brother

The Question

It's amazing how sometimes a simple decision can affect the rest of your life. Good decision, good result; bad decision, bad result.

It was a beautiful day in July a number of years ago when the new man in my life asked me an important question. I was very busy: working full-time, raising three children alone, running a household and I had just completed my degree part-time. My youngest child, adopted, had only been living with us for less than a year. The final paperwork hadn't even been done. And then there were the volunteer hours I was putting in.

I had just been asked by my employer to represent support staff at a national conference in Prince Edward Island in August. Never having been there, I jumped at the chance, all expenses paid.

It's not hard to figure out what that important question was. It unfolded like this. He said, "I've been a bachelor my whole life and I've decided there are good and bad things about being alone. The good thing is I can do whatever I want when I want to. The bad thing is that I don't have you with me. It's time to settle down. I've never met a woman like you before. And I've decided I want to spend the rest of my life with you. I love you with all my heart. Will you marry me?"

Even though I was very busy, without hesitation, I said "yes."

Then I started to think about it in the days that followed and I considered: what would my friends think? They hadn't even met him. What would my kids think? They were 11, 9 and 7. And what would my older brother say? He hadn't even checked him out yet.

So, I decided to ask the sage advice of my most trusted confidante, my beloved Granny. But, of course, she had died 5 years before. I had to, therefore, set off to the place that I visit often to reflect and talk through my problems. The graveyard.

It was a great summer day, sun shining, a squirrel scolding me from the pine tree that grows on our family plot. Quiet, except for that. And I sat on the ground and talked to my Granny, asking for her advice. I don't know what I expected. This was an important decision – a bolt of lightning, a burning bush? A loud voice from the sky? Or maybe just a mere whisper in the wind. But I didn't receive any of those signs.

Somewhat worried, I headed to the next best place to connect myself with my Granny: her family bible. Over the years, she had painstakingly written out in the first few pages who was related to whom, family generation after generation. The page ended with me. She never had time to inscribe my children's names.

I was looking for inspiration, for a sign. I figured that since she used to read this book often, it had part of her spirit attached to it. It is one of only two objects that belong to Granny that I inherited. And I was sure it was an object that was special to her. But, first, I had to carefully unwrap it from the tissue paper and the wide colourful ribbon that kept it dust free. I did so. Then I held the bible and closed my eyes. Still looking for a sign. Nothing. I turned different ways, holding it out in front of me. Still nothing. Not being a biblical scholar, I thought maybe I could flip the pages open at random and they would magically open to a spot or a passage that would tell me what I'm supposed to do.

So, I started flipping the pages. Flipping, flipping. Still nothing. Just then, a piece of paper fell out. It's an unusual shape. It drifted slowly, slowly to the floor. I hesitated just a moment, bent over and picked it up. It is the back of an envelope; the triangular part that you lick to seal the envelope, not the whole back. Just one little part. It is wrinkled and yellowed and it has some writing on it. I looked closely and recognized immediately the same scratchy handwriting that filled the first few pages of the bible in my hand. It is Granny's writing.

The words are simple. "Hold fast to those who truly love you, for they are few in a lifetime."

It's not signed or dated. I don't know if it's part of a poem, a passage from a book or a quote from a famous person. Maybe it's none of those things.

I do know my Granny just spoke to me.

I put the little slip of paper back in the bible, rewrap it carefully in the tissue paper and ribbon and return it to its special drawer.

And I say out loud, "Thank you, Granny."

In the next few days and weeks, Robert and I work on wedding plans. One hundred and fifty beautiful invitations are created with that quote as the first line. Lots of people ask me where I found such a wonderful sentiment. And I tell each of them, "I'm so glad you asked."

I'm sure that some people get inspiration or answers to their questions in sunsets or in other ways. My grandmother, who loved me so, reached across a vast amount of time and space to answer me.

And throughout the rest of my life, I will continue to watch for the signs.

My new husband and I have had a strong and happy married life together since June 8, 1991. Good decision, good result.

Thanks, Gran.

Sherry & Rob's Wedding Photo

"The Rain in Spain Falls Mainly on the Plain"
- Canadians posing as European tourists, Sherry on right.

Weather

Living in southern Ontario has always meant living in a pretty good climate for me. Yes, winter can be tough, but we're used to it. Summers can be hot, but we have lots of lakes. Fall is spectacular. Spring blooms and brings with it a promise of great weather ahead. We don't have to worry about flooding or tornadoes or tsunamis. We have fairly good weather. And we sort of wear, as a badge of honour, the fact that we live in Canada, the Great White North. We can wear no jacket in northern Florida or southern Alberta in just about any season. It takes more for us to feel cold than those not from Ontario. We're hardy.

Last April, I was in Vancouver. I went for a swim in the hotel pool outdoors. Chilly, but great after a long winter. One of the staff asked me if I was from Ontario or Quebec, where there's winter almost all the time. I had to tell them, we actually have seasons. And we hardly every have to use our dogsleds, especially in April.

Ontario's weather and location are not Vancouver's. Ah, Vancouver - majestic mountains, sparkling seas, absolutely breathtaking scenic drives. And the rain. The rain. It rains a lot. One thing I noticed on the first day I arrived, a beautiful sunny day, was that everyone carried an umbrella. Even the street people have umbrellas. Hmmm. I didn't know why, until day two and three and four and, yes, even day five. It rained or drizzled or misted, as the locals call it, every day. I decided I couldn't live here. The overcast skies and the incessant fog would drive me crazy. Give me a real change of seasons any day.

The rain also reminds me of a recent trip I took to Europe, billed as "Spain, Portugal and Germany in nine days." And what a nine-day trip it was, spent with six pseudo-strangers and two people I knew well. We had an amazing, rollicking good time. We had very little rain. The one time we did, we were on a walking tour in Piatro, a village in Portugal close to the ocean, known for its large number of seamen ready to work in those olden days. Their houses even had a ship marked on them. This told anyone looking for sea workers that at least one lived within.

We were heading across Spain on a long bus trip through large, flat areas with some spots of gently rolling hills. And very few trees, except for olive tress in neat groves. All I could see out of the bus window were green fields, hundreds of miles of them. The sun would intermittently break through the clouds. The raindrops continued to run down my bus window. And it was so beautiful and peaceful with hardly any towns and only one road cutting a clean ribbon through those green, grass-covered fields. I heard light snoring around me and knew that most of my fellow travellers were asleep or dozing. And out of nowhere came the voice of one of my sleepy travel mates. "Well, I guess that's it then. I know now it's true. The rain in Spain falls mainly on the plain." Laughter erupted, including the driver, whose English is not so good. We looked out our individual windows in time to see the clouds part, the sun shining through. The colour green was so blindingly green, just for a minute, on the plains of Spain on that day.

In the late spring or early winter in southern Ontario, the rain can often be mixed with wet snow and a stiff wind. Often that's the kind of poor weather that surrounds Remembrance Day, November 11th.

My father was a veteran, a man who proudly served in the Second World War: Private Irvin J. Douglas. He always took my mother and my younger sister and I to Remembrance Day services every year. He took out his medals that he kept in a special cupboard and shone them up to wear them each year at the same time.

My mother always dressed us up nicely, but warmly. She even tucked gloves into our pockets. I recall riding in the old brown, wood-panelled station wagon. With my father at the wheel, my mother was the passenger and two of us rode in the back. It's been many years now since our mother dressed us up for the special occasions. She died the year I turned 18. And even though my father is also long gone to the spirit world, I continue to attend Remembrance Day services each year as he would want me to.

Several years ago, November 11th dawned, cold, wet and windy. Of course, the brisk wind that day was from the north. I dressed warmly that morning knowing that the service would be held outside at the cenotaph next to the Rama United Church. About 30 people gathered in front of the little stone church on the south side of the monument facing north. I knew that at exactly 10:30 a.m., veterans and flag carriers and other dignitaries would march from the new community hall to the cenotaph for the service. This year, we only had three veterans left: George Charles,

Ken Simcoe Sr. and Leland Williams. With the wind howling and sleet coming down in sheets, the mournful sound of the bagpipes began. The bagpiper did not come every year, but I was always glad when he did. My dad always loved the sound of the pipes. Being a Douglas, he was proud that some of his ancestors came from Scotland long ago.

At any rate, through the sleet and the rain, they marched, flag bearers, colour guard, bagpiper and warriors. They marched in step, heads held high in dress uniforms and medals a little different on each person. And, although I had been focused on how cold and damp I felt, I was, at the same time, doing the math to figure out how old my father would be this year. He would be in his late 70s. I wondered if he would be able to walk alone. Would he use a cane or a wheelchair? The possibilities played through my mind.

Damn, I was cold. I pulled my winter gloves on tighter and stuffed my hands deeper into my pockets. I couldn't wait until the service was over. For sure, there would be a great lunch at the hall afterwards. There'd be corn soup and bannock and egg salad sandwiches on white bread. Yum! It would be my reward for standing in this lousy weather. Why couldn't they have this service in nice weather, like June I thought to myself? Yeah, June would be good. There were no other holidays in that month.

So, I'm concentrating on the cold today and the good weather to come and the sound of the bagpipes. I hadn't noticed that several dozen children from the school had walked down to the cenotaph with some of their teachers and a few parent volunteers. The teachers shushed them and gathered them around the west end of the memorial, kind of in a circle. I saw a couple of kids from Grade 1 and a bunch more from the higher grades, all the way up to Grade 6. I smiled, thinking how important it is to bring the children here for this service. I hope they're dressed warmly enough.

Everyone had arrived. The sound of the bagpipes wheezed to an end. The program indicated that we will now sing "O, Canada." So, we begin to sing together and the teachers join in. "O, Canada, our home and native land." I stop. The children are starting to sing, too. The tune is familiar, but the words aren't. I listen carefully. I strain to make out the words over the wind. The tune is "O, Canada" but the words are in Ojibway, Mnjikaning dialect. The children and their teachers, all together now and louder, are singing "O, Canada" in Ojibway. And I marvel at how much commitment and how many hours of practice it must have taken to teach them the words. Consider for a moment, the naysayers who thought building a school on the reserve was a bad idea. They said it would isolate our children, but no way would the school in town have taught them how to sing "O, Canada" in our language. And I know we did a good thing. Then the final verses are sung, some in English and some in Ojibway: "We stand on guard for thee." My father would be so proud. A single tear slips down my face and I forget about how cold I am.

After the wreaths are laid and prayers are said in both languages, everyone goes back to the hall for lunch. As anticipated, corn soup and bannock, egg salad sandwiches and even salmon sandwiches. I take the time, as I was taught so long ago, to shake hands with the veterans and ask how they are. They each call me by name. I am my father's daughter. Even though the children stay only a little while, just long enough for them to have a glass of juice before heading back to school, I make sure to shake each of their little hands and say "miigwech". I also speak to each teacher and thank them on behalf of my father, Private Douglas.

As I leave the hall that day and stand on the steps, I pull the collar of my coat up a little higher. It's still windy and rainy, but I don't feel quite as cold. Walking back to work, I smile again at the thought of our children learning our language at the same time they are being taught about Remembrance Day.

From the rain in Spain to Veterans' Day drizzle, I wonder what the weather forecast of the future holds for me.

The cenotaph next to the Rama United Church

To My Yet Unborn Grandson
from Gramma - December 2004

I've been waiting for you.
Because, you see,
I'm not so sure I did such a good job the first time around.
With my children, I mean.
One of them is your father.
I taught them how to swim.
I told them elders go first at the buffet table.
I showed them how to put a worm on a hook so it doesn't wiggle off.

I've been waiting for you.
Santa's Village™, Wonderland™, lawn sales,
Kraft Dinner™, dollar stores, Fleecy™ sheets.
All the things you'll need to know.
There'll be some work, of course.
But, also lots of walking and talking.
Telling stories, mugs and hugs and laughter.

I've been waiting for you.
And when I think I've done a poor job of raising my children…
I realize my daughter makes the best bannock of anyone I know.
Besides which, she's bright, a voracious reader
and checks in on her grandmother.

I've been waiting for you.
And when I think I've done an adequate job of raising my children…
I find out my son listens almost exclusively to pow-wow music

in his truck.
His friends think he's strange.
But I know he's funny and kind and
animals and women really like him.
My life is truly blessed.

I've been waiting for you.
And I think about the times I've braided my daughter's hair
as she got ready to dance.
And I think about the evening I helped my son make
tobacco ties for his friend's funeral.
And together many times,
my children and I have pored through photo albums of people
Long gone to the spirit world, who continue to watch over us.
I know that some day my children will teach their children
how the "photo album people" are related to us.

I've been waiting for you.
And what title might you give me?
Nana, Gramma, Nanny, Gran-Gran, Granny, Grammy, Nookomis…

I've been waiting for you.
You have so much to teach me.

Sherry's Grandson, Paxton.

Uncle Terry

He was born the youngest child of Mary and Joe Monette in Toronto in late March 1933. They named him Terrance. But to me, he was just Uncle Terry and sometimes Uncle Tub. He never married, though when I was older, he told me about several of the great loves of his life, according to him, "the ones who got away."

I have many, many fond memories of my mother's brother. Her nickname for him was "Schnookie." I still don't know why. Many people described my uncle as eccentric. Not knowing what that meant as a small child, Uncle Terry represented love and fun to me. In later years, I though my Uncle Terry was cool.

Granny Monette, my mother's and Uncle Terry's mother, lived three houses away from the train crossing at Longford Mills. She called her little ramshackle creaky house the Sugar Shack for some unknown reason. We never harvested maple syrup there. My mother would often say, "Sherry Lynn, ride your bike to the sugar shack. Your Granny wants to visit", and I would. Uncle Terry would be there. He never lived with anyone else, but his mother.

Every day of the year, without fail, a CN passenger train would travel clickety clack across the tracks at Longford Mills at 3:20 p.m. sharp. In the summer months and on weekends, if I were visiting, Uncle Terry would say "Hurry up, the train's coming soon." When I was really little, he would carry me the short distance to the tracks on his shoulders. Right on time at 3:20 p.m. the train would go roaring by. Clickety clack, clickety clack. We would wave like crazy people. The conductor in his striped cap would blow the horn: whoo-hoooo! We would keep waving and the passengers would wave back. It was a great thrill. After the train went by, Uncle Terry would take me to the old general store, just over the tracks. It looked like one of those buildings in the old west, with a porch and a peaked roof at the front. It had wooden floors and a long wooden counter with stools with a brass footrest running the length of the counter. On top were large glass jars with removable glass tops filled with peppermint and bubble gum and licorice. I could pick one thing and Uncle Terry would pay for it. My dentist today would thank him. They were the best of times.

Even now, as an adult who drives, being stopped at a railway crossing for a passenger train to go by reminds me of my Uncle Terry. I smile to myself as I hear him say, "Hurry up!" Clickety clack, clickety clack.

Before the millennium year, the CN and CP railway lines were abandoned and torn up throughout southern Ontario. It seems that rail travel and shipping by train had fallen out of favour as too expensive, slow and labour intensive.

I recently found myself out for a drive stopped at the old rail crossing at Longford Mills. I was wishing for that 3:20 p.m. train and reliving those happy times with my beloved uncle. It's too bad my grandchildren will never experience the same thing.

My Uncle Terry was a great dancer, especially for a man so large. Not very tall, perhaps 5 foot 5, he was quite rotund. I never knew him as a young man, but I'm told he served two years in the Canadian Navy and was positively svelte. The Uncle Terry I remember weighed about 200, maybe 220. He was always slightly balding, but kept his fine hair long enough at the back to flip up.

During that time, there used to be regular weekend dances at the Longford Community Centre. Sometimes, in those early days, there was a live band playing, but, more often, it was a DJ. No matter, my Uncle Terry could dance to anything: swing, jive and rock. He was a really accomplished ballroom dancer. My uncle was fastidious about how he looked, maybe because of his time in the service. His shirts were always well fitted. His pants, often cuffed, always had a crisp crease. He wore a belt, a good watch and leather wingtip shoes. Many times Uncle Terry would ask me to dance. I was shy, clumsy and afraid that I would fall on my face and people would laugh at me. He persisted. I relented. And since he was such a strong partner, I followed my Uncle Terry's lead and actually glided around the floor, weaving in and out of other couples, never coming close to crashing into anyone. Right in step, perfectly in tune, me and Uncle Terry. He was such a great dancer, he convinced me that I was one, too. Many times, when the music ended, dancers would stop and applaud. I always thought they were clapping for us. Although I'm still not a good dancer, I recall with great fondness those days when my Uncle Terry made me believe I could do anything.

Uncle Terry also played the harmonica, or mouth organ, as my mother called it. Whether he was dressed up or casual, the harmonica was a permanent fixture in his right pants pocket. He was really good at playing, too, and told me one time when he was a young man in Toronto "I jammed with the guys in the band." I never knew what band he meant, but it only solidified my belief in Uncle Terry's coolness.

When I was 11 or 12 years old, my father became Chief of our small community. About the same time, my father's brother-in-law, my Uncle Terry, got a job with the Union of Ontario Indians as Treasurer. It turns out that although never formally trained, my Uncle Terry was a wizard with numbers. People say he could figure out your income tax refund in his head. His figuring was always within $5.00 of the final correct number. A real gift.

I often travelled with my father to Chiefs' meetings, both in Ontario and beyond. During my years as a young teenager, both my Uncle Terry and my father were often at the same political meetings. I remember one meeting, in particular, my first time in Sault Ste. Marie; my Uncle Terry was standing at the front presenting financial data to hundreds of people. White shirt, pressed pants, matching belt and shoes and even suspenders. Very buttoned down. He had the overhead projector on, with rows and rows of numbers. Uncle Terry talked on. And on. I began to nod off. I wasn't the only one. More than once, my father nudged me to keep me awake. Then it seemed like Uncle Terry was done his presentation.

"And that left a grand total remaining for this quarter of $1.64", announced my uncle. There was a silence. "Any questions?" Still silence. Awkward silence.

Then one of the oldest chiefs stood up at the back of the large meeting room. "Mr. Treasurer, what did you do with that $1.64?"

"I bought stamps", Uncle Terry shot back.

Everyone roared. My father smiled. We broke for lunch.

When I became a young mother in the late 1970s, my husband and I joined the Sunday night bowling league to have a break from the kids. One Sunday morning, we got a call that one teammate was sick. We needed to find a last-minute replacement. I called friends, relatives, co-workers, neighbours, just about everyone I knew. Exasperated, I figured we'd have to default. Then I suggested to my husband that we call Uncle Terry.

Always contrary in those days, my husband said, "No way. He won't know how to bowl." Finally, he said, "All right, what do we have to lose?" We picked up Uncle Terry because he never did learn how to drive. As usual, we had three games to bowl. I worried about how our team would fare with Uncle Terry as our fourth. As it turned out, I needn't have worried.

You remember those old Flintstones cartoons, the ones with Barney and Fred on a bowling team? Not the Loyal Order of the Buffalo ones, the ones where Fred Flintstone actually bowled. He would pick up the ball, rise on his toes and walk tippy-toe-like to the line, pull his arm back, then send the ball down the alley. Pow! A strike! In those cartoons, Fred was called Tippy Toes Flintstone. That's exactly how Uncle Terry bowled. And it was strike. After strike. After strike.

In non-competitive league bowling, it is common to scratch the low score in each game. Being a decent bowler, that hardly ever happened to me. I was on an award-winning bowling league in college. On this night, in particular, it was my husband's plight to be scratched not once, not twice, but three times. My Uncle Terry (Do ya think he can bowl?), last minute stand-in, bowled not one, not two, but three perfect games. It had never occurred at that alley before or as I understand it, since. Partway through game two, most of the other teams stopped bowling. They ordered a hot dog from the snack bar, bought a coke and sat down to watch. People were shouting, applauding and cheering. My Uncle Terry, in his characteristic modest way, nervously ran his fingers through his hair and up over that flip at the back and acknowledged his new friends and fans.

My Uncle substituted on bowling teams many times after that night. A fairly good bowler, he never duplicated that night. He never bowled another perfect game. But, for those few hours, my single unemployed Uncle Terry in his forties, who still lived at home with his mother, was a star, a celebrity. Everyone wanted to know who he was and where he came from. Strangers slapped him on the back and shook his hand. I was happy and proud to introduce him simply as my Uncle Terry.

After my Grandmother died, my Uncle Terry slipped a little. He was lonely. He drank more. He could no longer do math in his head. He couldn't hold a job. He continued to live in my Granny's old house and lived on disability. He loved our visits. I often rode my bike the two miles to the sugar shack to see him. He was always so glad to see me. He made me tea; he played the harmonica; he told me stories.

His old brown radio on the shelf above the woodstove was tuned to oldies music. His house was sparsely furnished and the floor tiles were worn. But it was warm with love and kindness and fine memories.

I remember the last Hallowe'en I went trick or treating with my sister. I was in Grade 9. I was 13. It was definitely the last year for me to go door to door and ask for candy. My mother worked as a nurse and she was at work that evening. My brother, Mark, 10 years older, was in charge. He gave us our pillowcases and our flashlights and told us to be back by 8. Off we went, happily getting a sack full of goodies from people we knew.

Even though there were only eight houses on the Longford Mills Road, those eight houses would get us closer to the sugar shack. By 7:30, we set out down that road, tired, but excited with all our loot and especially glad to visit Uncle Terry.

The porch light was on and there was a 50-50 chance Granny would be in the city visiting. After knocking for some time with no response, we peeked in the window. Uncle Terry was on the couch. We knocked louder and called his name. Finally, he answered, disheveled and bleary eyed. In retrospect, he must have been drinking.

Uncle Terry invited us in, glad for the company. He seemed surprised that it was Hallowe'en. He wasn't prepared. He had no candy, he said. He rifled through the drawers and kitchen cupboards. Nothing. He apologized. Then he snapped his fingers. He had an idea. There, on top of the fridge, he found two bananas. With a flourish, he placed one in each of our bulging pillowcases and sent us home. We made it back just about 8 o'clock.

My brother dumped out our pillowcases to "check our candy". I know now it was to take any Smarties© or black licorice, which he loved. The bananas tumbled out. He picked up one in each hand and said, "Ah, I see Uncle Terry was home." I never did ask him how he knew.

The years passed and Uncle Terry grew frailer and less lively. He had a difficult time controlling his diabetes. He lived for a time, not just with my brother and his family, but with ours. Although his health was failing, he always thanked us for driving him here and there. He always appreciated whatever I cooked for him. My kids adored their Great Uncle Terry. He always had lots of stories. He always kept loose change in his pocket to hand out to children as required. We loved him so.

Terrance Monette died on July 25, 2001 at Longford Mills, surrounded by friends and family.

Although single to the end, I know my Uncle Terry had a good life. My memories of my dear uncle involved trains and swing music and bowling shoes. I still pass through the produce section of the grocery store and smile when I see the bananas.

Thank you Uncle Terry, for all that you were to my family and me. You continue to live on in my memories and my heart and, now, in my stories. I will never forget you.

Read at Literary Lapses Festival, Leacock Home, Orillia, Ontario, August 11, 2006

Sherry's Uncle Terry

Three Months

"Three months", she announced with great excitement on that January day. "We'll have our own place in thee months at most." It seems availability and references had finally converged in our little community all at once.

Our grandson, Paxton, and his mother had been living with us since Easter. A series of unfortunate events had left her and our only grandchild virtually without a good place to live. Of course, we took them in, temporarily.

We had to rearrange our lives. Empty nesters, we were. Our last child left over five years ago. Our grown children, ages 27, 25 and 22, had gone off on their own, as children as supposed to do. Baby Paxton Scott Edward (our older son is the father) was born five days before Christmas by caesarian section last year, which makes him over one year old now.

And, just after Easter, Pax and his mom moved in and basically took over our lives and our home. There were bottles and soothers, diapers and liquid Tylenol™, sleepers and bath oil for babies. As Pax grew, there was so much stuff: car seats and strollers, trucks and musical toys, blankets and a crib, CDs and movies, and a mountain of laundry each day.

Paxton walked early at eight months, but seems to be a slow talker. His clearest word is "gog" which is short for "dog." Elvis, our bichon frise, is his best friend, even though Elvis had never met anyone shorter than four feet tall in his entire dog life. They chase each other around, they often eat from the same dish, they even bark at the same things.

And we, before we knew what was happening, became transformed from very contented empty nesters to often-frazzled grandparents.

Robert married me as a very simple man over 40 when my children were 8, 10 and 12. He has been a remarkable husband and father with little practice. He is kind and loving. He is clear when he needs to be and he often needed to be with my three teenagers. He is my port in a storm and my biggest fan.

And just as we're getting used to being alone and travelling when we want, eating and sleeping late and sometimes making milk shakes at ten at night, because we can, we became grandparents.

I don't want to seem like I'm complaining about the most exciting, busy and actually exhilarating year of my life. I was a good mom, but I am a fabulous grandmother.

Pax's mother is a very good single mom and a college student to boot. I've taught this young 22-year old how to shop and cook and separate whites from colours. I've talked her down at 3:00 a.m. when Paxton's temperature soared to 103. I helped plan a first birthday party that would put Martha Stewart to shame – 50 invited guests, fresh flowers, caterers and a photographer and even a visit from Santa.

We have settled into a routine, the four of us. I pick Pax up at 4:40 on Mondays from the babysitter's and I sing songs to him all the way home. He always laughs and claps his hands when I'm done. I feed him whatever was left over from Sunday dinner. He is a good eater. I bathe him in the kitchen sink almost every night, using lavender to calm him. I help do his laundry and fold his cute little clothes and sort his miniature socks. I spend hours with him in the pool. He cries every time I take him out. I read to him and sing nursery school songs from memory.

And I love him more than I ever thought possible. I had a busy, rewarding life with great freedom before Pax moved in. I didn't think life could be better, but it can and it is.

Paxton is described by our only daughter as a "one-man party in a box". His eyes actually sparkle. He is fair-haired and has his mother's dimples. Should he need to wear eyeglasses some day, his eyelashes will brush the glass. He laughs easily and smiles often. He is truly a delight.

And what of Paxton and his grandpa? They play trucks and make vroom-vroom car noises. They wrestle and often fall off the couch doing so. They share ice-cold water in sippy cups. Pax loves the sound of the ice dispenser and will come running from wherever he is when he hears the ice "clink, clink" into the glass. My husband has adapted well to his new role.

And in three months when they move, how will I survive? Who will I sing to? Will you walk into my garden, said the spider to the fly? Will my lavender scented bubbles go to waste? Will our icemaker overflow with ice chips due to non-use?

A dear friend of mine, upon learning that our grandson was moving in nine months ago, clapped her hands together in delight. She gave me some advice. She said, "A grandchild is a true blessing. How wonderful he will live with you, if only for a little while. Cherish each day. You never know how long it might last. His mother might get another job, move away, fall in love and they'll be gone. Make each day count."

I never understood why songs or poems aren't written about grandchildren. They are so amazing. They represent unconditional love, with no strings attached. They evoke emotions unlike most other things in life.

A blessing, indeed. It seems Paxton and his mother are not moving a country or a province away. They will be one mile down the road. We'll be able to pick up Pax whenever we miss him or our life is simply too quiet.

Make each day count. I shall. Three months will fly by as will our years with this engaging, funny, wonderful child.

I can't wait for the next chapter to unfold.

Paxton & his "Gampa"

Irvin Douglas paid as an Indian Guide in the French River area - circa 1965

Old George

I recall attending that community meeting in 1972 as clearly as if it were yesterday. Unemployment was rampant in my community of Mnjikaning in those days, often with 85% of members out of work year-round.

The community was called together that spring to discuss our options. One person suggested we cut down trees and sell the firewood. Others said there was work in the London area coming up in the tobacco fields. One elder suggested we needed to keep our children in school so they could go to college or university and then get jobs. A middle-aged grandmother said we needed nurses and teachers. Someone (I don't know who) wrote down these suggestions on the rolling blackboard (actually, it was green).

I was sitting between my Granny Douglas and my mother. I remember so well when a distinguished middle-aged man stood up to speak near the end. Granny whispered to me, "That's Old George." He didn't look old to me, I thought. Granny must have read my mind. She whispered, "That's Old George because he's older than Young George. Listen." I nodded as if I understood.

Old George wore a crisp white shirt and dress pants perfectly creased. He had on black loafers. He used his hands when he talked. "Ah-niin. Most of you know me. I'm George St. Germain, businessman, pilot, entrepreneur. I've been listening closely to the discussion this evening. And I almost don't want to say it, but I had a dream. A dream that showed every one in this community prospering, from the young to the old - new cars, nice houses, a paved road, safe drinking water." Old George hesitated. Everyone listened politely.

"And I keep thinking about this dream because it was so clear. In the dream, we had built a casino in Rama." There was muttering around the room. "That's right, a casino, right here. Lots of visitors poured through the doors in my dream. They all left their money at our Indian casino".

The person who had been writing on the blackboard said, "George, you know there are no casinos in our area. I don't think they're allowed." He held the piece of chalk in his hand, fiddling with it nervously as he spoke.

"I know that, I know." Old George's voice was stronger now. "But I know we have a lot of smart people in this community. They could go to the government and negotiate in good faith, convince the government to let us open an Indian casino right here. It will solve our unemployment problem. We can do it. Think about it." Old George sat down.

There was more whispering and muttering around the room. My mother said softly, almost under her breath, "Never happen." The person wielding the chalk at the front added "Indian casino" to the list with two question marks after it.

When the meeting was over, there was coffee and tea and sandwiches - egg salad, my favourite. We drove home in the old station wagon. My father drove, but he hadn't been sitting with us at the meeting. When I cast my mind back on that time, I think he was kind of running the meeting that night. No matter. I don't know what happened to that list on the blackboard. Probably more than one community meeting was held to discuss our community's unemployment woes. And they weren't solved with just one idea.

I didn't know Old George in 1972, but, I came to know him in 1990 when we both applied for a job with the Ontario government. I learned he was a kind man, a gentleman, a man in his 60s with both his bus licence and pilot's licence. A painter of houses, a man with opinions. A person who smoked like a chimney and enjoyed fine dining. Old George was a risk-taker, an astute businessman, a community member and volunteer. And I know now that Old George was not just a dreamer, but a prophet as well.

On July 31, 1996, Casino Rama opened its doors. Ontario's only First Nations commercial casino is a strong economic engine for the entire region, welcoming, cn average, 13,000 visitors a day. But it didn't happen instantly. There were many meetings with all levels of government, politicking of the highest order and negotiating sessions that went on long into the night. Some describe Casino Rama in 2007 as the country's most successful casino, employing more Native people in one spot than any other business in Canada.

Casino Rama revenues have helped Mnjikaning build a school, seniors complex, fire hall, police station and daycare centre. Everyone who is able to work is working. There are lots of new vehicles in the driveways of new houses. The water is finally fit to drink.

Long before opening, a cultural advisory committee was struck to advise the Casino Rama project on large and small details of external and internal design. Pipe-carriers, language keepers, artists, elders and youth gave thought to copper wall sconces, the use of the fish weirs motif and the placement of large water features. Visitors are in awe of the striking, yet comfortable, place that is Casino Rama. Yes, a gambling emporium, but also a visual celebration of the Chippewa culture that lives on in the new millennium.

And what about Old George, the seer who saw the future and chose to share his dream during a time when the community thought they needed an action plan? Old George died of cancer mere months before Casino Rama opened. It was a great loss to his family and our community. To honour him, the community named its high-end steakhouse "St. Germain's" after Old George.

Old George was the kind of person who appreciated a fine meal. St. Germain's Steakhouse has been described as the best steakhouse north of Toronto. The restaurant has a fireplace, open kitchen, lots of copper and comfortable seating. It's a place to sit with friends and family and experience a truly exceptional meal with outstanding service.

Old George would be pleased. Every time I walk past St. Germain's, I think fondly of him.

Sometimes, when we are going through a dark and difficult time, we need to get together and make a plan that involves clear and decisive action. And, sometimes, just sometimes, we need to take a few minutes to just sit back and for only a little while, listen to a dreamer.

George St. Germain
"Old George"

Stop at the Mall

I often wonder why I stayed in this little town. I had job offers elsewhere, but I stayed here. It's actually a city, but no-one thinks of it that way. Now, Toronto is a city; Orillia is still a town.

And then the most amazing thing happened. I realized why I like it here.

I was driving Dave to the mall - an ordinary job to be sure, mundane really. And as I pulled into the mall parking lot, I reminded myself of how small the mall is and how the selection often leaves something to be desired. And I dream, just for a moment, of my next all-day shopping trip to the 'Big Smoke'. Maybe in April, when the weather is better.

And, as usual, the outside of the mall is pretty deserted. One person is loading groceries into his trunk. An elderly woman with a big paisley scarf wrapped around her head and her wool coat is hurrying into the main door of the Orillia Square Mall.

I sit there in my car for just a moment after Dave goes inside. I watch a young father, a tall young man, maybe 21 or 22, pushing a shopping cart along the sidewalk, just freshly cleared of all snow. He is walking quickly. I would say at quite a brisk speed. And a little boy, maybe two years old, blonde and blue-eyed, with a navy snowsuit with red boots and light blue mittens, most likely the man's young son, but not too tall, chubby really. The little boy is standing up in the cart, facing ahead, holding onto the rim. I see his mittens attached to strings flapping in the wind. He looks happy, but somehow terrified at the same time. Excited, but apprehensive. Exhilarated, perhaps. Yes, that's the right word, exhilarated. And he holds on tight with his little fat fingers, white-knuckled, as his father pushes the cart quickly over bumps and cracks in the sidewalk. And there is no one else around.

The smile on his little face goes from ear to ear.

As did mine.
Couldn't do that at a Toronto mall.

I've Been Shot At!
What's Your Excuse?

He didn't mean to shoot at me. It just happened.

I was seven, maybe eight. I know that because I could stand in the kitchen where the cupboards meet coming from opposite ends near the stove. I could stand with my back to the lower cupboards, put one hand on the counter on the left and one hand on the counter on the right. If I tried really hard, I could lift myself up in the air and do a little ballet move. If I did it too many times, my hands and wrists would go numb, the way your mouth can feel after getting freezing at the dentist.

So, I was standing in that corner, practising my ballet moves that I just knew I would never get to use in real life. My mother was working as usual. It was night-time, summertime. I was the only kid at home. The rest were all grownups there that night. The grownups in our house that night were all males. One was my father. They were playing poker at the old Formica™ kitchen table, the four of them. I think one might have been Kenny Snache. I don't remember who the other two were. The light bulb screwed into the socket on the ceiling seemed bright. None of the light it cast was flattering to anyone.

Sometimes it was kind of interesting watching the poker game. Most times it wasn't. From my vantage point, I could only see the cards of the one unknown person with his back to me. He held up his cards from time to time in front of his face. It seemed that cards with faces on them were the best kind to have. Things seemed to be going well for the stranger. There were large piles of money on the table that the stranger had raked to his side of the table as the hands were played.

The pile of money was pretty high again. Someone said "Call!" I don't know what happened next because it was all so fast. My father, facing me, in one fluid motion, pushed back his chair, stood up, reached his right hand across his chest and pulled out a gun. "Cheater!" he screamed.

Stubby beer bottles crashed to the floor. The other two players were on their feet. The stranger remained seated for some unknown reason. The gun was pointed at the stranger and, in effect, at me. The gun went off with a thunderous crack. My ears were ringing. There was the acrid smell of gunpowder in the air. I suppose the combination of the late hour, the beer and a game that required some brain acuity after several hours, all led to one thing. Something was going to go wrong.

The bullet meant for the cheating stranger missed him. Fortunately, it also missed me. But not by much. I think I must have been trying to lift myself off the floor, ballet-style, at the exact moment my father pulled the trigger. Otherwise, the bullet would have gone into my elbow, hip or maybe even my heart. Instead, the bullet passed harmlessly to my left through the pots and pans cupboard and into the furnace. The bullet went into the plywood about 1 ½ inches from my father's second daughter, me.

By the time I had figured this all out, the stranger was gone. So were the other two poker players, which left a lot of spilled beer, the smell of gunpowder and the light from a single light bulb casting its bright light on a really big pile of money in the middle of the old Formica™ table.

My mother came home about 7 the next morning. I had long gone to bed. My father was asleep, snoring loudly. The Colt .45 was still on the table, sitting in a puddle of beer. My mother woke me up to find out what had happened the night before. She didn't think it was as cool as I did, that I'd been shot at. My mother yelled at my father for most of the day. She stomped around, ranted and raved, slammed doors and told my father he was stupid. She even went, at one point, into the furnace room to look for the bullet. She never did find it. Everyone thought it went right inside the furnace and is probably still there.

After that, I was never allowed to stay home alone with my father when my mother worked nights. I could stay with my younger sister and older brother in the house with my father. I guess the logic was: What were the chances he could shoot two of us?

Decades later, I attended a session (with 300 other people) with a motivational speaker. The brochure promised we would see the world differently after his presentation. I don't know if that happened for the other 299 people, but it certainly happened for me. In the first five minutes, the speaker asked everyone to stand up. He then asked everyone who had never been shot at, to sit down.

One man and I were the only two to remain standing. The speaker said "I won't embarrass you two by asking you to tell your story. It doesn't matter. You're still here. You and you (he pointed to me) have been saved for something special. You have something important to do with your life. I'm sure of that and you should be, too."

We sat down and the speaker continued on for about an hour. I'm not sure what he talked about. I just remember the first five minutes.

Growing up in a home with alcoholic parents can be a dangerous place for a child. Most children survive. Some don't. None are unscathed. Some carry visible scars; many more, invisible ones.

Since the bullet missed me, I guess I fall into that "invisible scars" category. And I'm still here.

My father didn't mean to shoot at me. It just happened.

Sherry as a young girl, note outhouse in background

Orillia Public Library circa 1979

My Public Library

My grandmother loved me so. I know this because she introduced me to the public library at a very early age.

My childhood was a poor one. We didn't get proper running water until I was thirteen. Often, there wasn't enough food to make a real meal. I remember getting dressed many times in front of the open oven door because we had run out of heating oil.

My grandmother's house was always a safe, warm place. Although she probably had less money than our family had, I suppose she had learned to 'make do'. My Granny's house had books and magazines and even newspapers. I was surrounded by stories there. She taught me to treat all books with respect. "Don't fold down the corners. Be careful not to crack open the spine too far. And never, ever write in a book."

My Granny loved me enough to hire a ride to take us to town one day. She took me to the Orillia Public Library, an old brick building in downtown Orillia. I remember holding her hand as I looked up at stacks and stacks of books, hundreds and thousands of them. Picture books, animal books, The Green Fairy Book.

I was allowed to take six books home with me, after Granny helped me get a library card. They asked my name and what school I attended. I had to print my name on the line. Granny told me to keep my card in a special space. I could use it anytime to get more books. I was seven years old.

And so began a lifetime of reading and loving the printed word. Most Saturdays I dusted, I washed floors, I cut grass, anything to raise the bus fare. It cost twenty-five cents to ride the bus into town. At the library, I traded in my books for different ones, week after week, month after month, year after year.

As time went on, my dog-eared library card changed from paper to heavier paper and, more recently, to plastic. Granny sat patiently as I read for her for hours on end. She loved me so.

My Granny taught me the value of a public library. In retrospect, it changed my life. I even went to college and studied library science, graduating with honours. My love affair with public libraries continues.

My Grandmother passed away more than 20 years ago, but, even now, whenever I enter the library, I think of her. In Granny's memory, every year on her birthday, I donate money to the public library for them to buy books. I ask that a bookplate be inserted into each book, which reads, "In memory of Granny Douglas, who loved me so."

Perhaps, right now, there is a small child who has borrowed one of those special books from the same library. Maybe, they are reading from its pages right this minute. I imagine a little girl reading for hours to someone who loves her, just like my Granny loved me.

Submitted Spring 2007 to
Province of Ontario contest on "Public Libraries in Ontario
- How They Have Affected our Lives"
(500 words or less).

Granny's Pitcher

Sometimes in life, there is an object, a thing, that represents a person and that stands for the unconditional love of that person. In my case, that thing is a beat-up old English pitcher, multi-coloured, with barely-discernible people on it.

When I was a little girl, I spent a great deal of time with my Granny, in our language, Nookomis. My father's mother must have been a little wild when she was younger. After all, she had my father out of wedlock when she was barely 20. My Granny never married. I have pictures of her as a young woman, dressed as a flapper: ¾ length dress, no sleeves, ribbon trim, flat shoes, a knit hat fitting her head closely and two extra-long strands of pearls. She had a wonderful singing voice. Granny played the piano, speakeasy-style. She told me once she learned to drive on one of those old cars you had to wind up at the front. She had beautiful red hair and, over the course of her lifetime, several great loves. Granny could say "I love you" in seven languages. I think she was a bit of a rebel.

My Granny lived in a creaky two-storey, white clapboard house on the main road on the hill in downtown Rama. I spent a lot of time there.

Childhood memories of the old English pitcher tell me the jug had multiple uses: in the summer, it held lemonade we had mixed together from fresh lemons. Sometimes, it held iced tea, not the kind you make today from the pre-bought mix, but the real thing. Also, in the warm summer months, the jug often held purple lilacs from Granny's giant lilac bush that grew right up against the house on the south side. In later years, the pitcher held white peonies, plucked from the little bush on the north side of the house. I loved those peonies, so fragrant and big. I helped Granny transplant that bush from the Simcoe house next door. They were tearing down the old Simcoe homestead to build a newer, safer, more modern house. Granny commandeered me after school one spring day to move the plant to her property. She said next door it would just die because of all the construction, so it might as well have a new home. I think we stole that peony bush.

But the fragrance year after year was lovely. They always looked so cheerful in the old English pitcher, sitting on the wooden kitchen table with the sunlight streaming through Granny's old rippled glass window. The peonies practically spilled out of the pitcher, the blooms were so lush. Many times I ate at Granny's table, admiring those flowers, studying the millions of pointy white petals.

After Granny's old house was torn down, replaced with a simple one-storey, two-bedroom bungalow, the English pitcher continued to hold old-fashioned lemonade and iced tea for Granny and me. The peonies and lilacs did not survive the construction in Granny's yard. It was too bad. In her new house, the jug most recently held wooden spoons, sitting on the gleaming kitchen counter next to the new electric stove.

My Granny lived into her early 80s, living alone in her little house, listening to Rusty Draper on the radio every morning. She loved to watch "The Honeymooners" and "I Love Lucy" on her floor model black and white TV. As the years went on, her daily walks became shorter. Cataract surgery, osteoporosis and high blood pressure took their toll. I visited my Granny often. She especially loved feeding digestive cookies to my children. A simple woman, leading a simple life.

There came a day when Granny realized she needed to move into a nursing home. She was frail and not eating properly. She insisted that we not pack up any of her furniture or other things. She would be back. The move to the nursing home was temporary, just for the winter.

It was that Christmas, all those years ago, that Granny gave me the best present possible. The lemonade pitcher was carefully wrapped in an old lace curtain, set inside a brown paper shopping bag from the butcher's. As I unwrapped it, Granny said simply, "I want you to have it." I cried. Granny beamed.

Despite Granny's eternal optimism, the move to the nursing home was not temporary. Granny never came home again.

My Granny's old jug, chipped, well-loved and made in England, has a special place in my home.

For me, it holds the warm memories of a hot summer day. It reminds me of fresh-squeezed lemons and sweet iced tea, shared in tall mismatched glasses, as we visited at the kitchen table. And, today, when I fill the vase with flowers of any kind, the love of my Granny again surrounds me.

It's a simple thing really, a decorative object that to most people doesn't deserve a second glance. But it means the world to me and it always will.

I will be sure to tell my grandchildren about their great, great

Grandmother.

Granny as a young woman at the "old house".

Sherry (holding fish) with sister and mother

Just Like My Childhood

The last time it happened was on a sunny fall day. Actually, the first frost had come and gone, so, officially, it was Indian Summer.

My youngest son wanted to go to the roller rink, where all the other kids hung out on weekends. I hesitated. Was he old enough? He would be with his new friend, Corey. Finally, I relented. It seemed safe.

I arrived two hours later, as scheduled, to pick up my son, but there was something different about him. Something wrong. His usual smiling mouth was sullen. The sparkle in his eyes was missing. His hair was matted to his head, not just with sweat. It was dirty and sticky.

"What's wrong? What happened?" I had to say it twice before he spoke. When he did, the truth just came tumbling out.

An older child started it. He called him a "dirty Indian." Then a "no-good wagon-burner." And when that wasn't enough, after he pushed him down, he spit on him. The other children thought this looked like fun and joined in.

As I heard this story, I was reminded of my own childhood, not the exact same tale, but similar. I was transported back to those early days of mine spent at David H. Church School in Orillia. Most of those kids hated me, I was sure. Well, actually, they didn't like any of those Rama children who rode "the Indian bus" and I was one of them. They made fun of how we dressed and talked. They especially loved to humiliate us, poking us, pinching us, teasing my friends about their long, shaggy hair.

One day, Mary (I can't recall her last name) got hold of Phillip's lunch in the school yard. She ripped open the bag and inspected his sandwich. "Ewww!" she announced to the world. "What is that? It doesn't even look like meat. Yech! It smells bad!" Kids held me back so I couldn't reach Mary to wipe that smirk off her face. "Leave him alone!" I squeaked.

Mary turned to me. "What's wrong? Your boyfriend can't stick up for himself?" Everyone laughed. Mary dropped Phillip's sandwich on the ground and kicked dirt on top of it. I thought the lard sandwich looked pretty good, considering how much we had eaten that day. In fact, lunch would have been our first meal of the day. The mob let go of both me and Phillip at the same time. We fell to our knees.

"I'm telling!" I croaked. My friend, eyes looking at me beseechingly, looked beaten.

"No, you won't," he whispered. He was right. The beatings only got worse if we tattled.

My mind flashed back to the present with me holding my son's shoulders, both of us in the front seat, car running, as I try to get the details out of him.

"It's okay, Mom," he said quietly.

"No, it's not!" I scream. "It'll never be okay."

I looked into my son's beautiful brown eyes and I thought about his usually shiny jet black hair and I admired his flawless burnished skin, now tear-stained. I wanted to gather him up in my arms, tell him it'll be all right and chase away the hurt for good.

I was so angry, I was shaking! How dare they do that to my very special 8-year old, whose quiet kindness and endearing sense of humour is remembered by everyone he meets. And I wanted to hurt those children who made this little boy feel so bad. I looked suspiciously at each child leaving the roller rink that day. "Was it him? What about her?" He couldn't remember.

Later, after I bathed my son and helped him comb his hair, we looked in the mirror together. I said, "All better?" And he smiled again. I said, "You know that what those children did was wrong. And mean. And you don't deserve it. Lots of people love you. Remember that. Especially me."

And he put his small arms around my neck and hugged me tight. And I silently promised myself I'd protect my son from all those ignorant people. As long as I could.

Lake St. John

My father had heard that trespassers were back on our property on nearby Lake St. John: drinking, partying and leaving a mess behind. To my 8-year old mind, I wasn't sure what trespassers were, but they sounded bad. My father told me that on Saturday I would go with him to the other lake to put up some signs to keep people out. I recall word-for-word what the signs said:

"NOTICE - this is an Indian Reserve. Any person caught trespassing will be subject to a fine of not more than two thousand dollars or imprisonment for a term of six months, or both. By order of the Indian Agent."

Mom would have to pack us a lunch and I would have to wear a hat, pants and long sleeves because of the bugs and poison ivy.

I was excited that spring day. I loved going to the other lake. It would be some time alone with my dad, who always seemed to be so busy, acting as a fishing guide for those Toronto people or selling minnows and leeches from his small roadside business. We would ride in the little aluminum boat. He would trust me to jump out right at the shore and tie up the rope to either a rock or a tree, so the boat wouldn't float away.

The appointed Saturday came. Our lunch was packed. I was properly dressed. It wasn't too hot. Good! My head wouldn't be too sweaty.

I always liked the sound of the aluminum boat going through the water. The motor was humming away and sometimes the waves would bang on the metal. It was a pleasing sound as we headed due east.

We were getting closer and my father expertly wove his way past the exposed rocks in the shallow lake. We had to go through the high reeds and the bulrushes that grew in the low area before we reached shore. I was in the very front of the boat on this beautiful day. My father told me to watch for rocks and warn him if I saw any. Our speed slowed and minutes crept by. I watched for rocks.

Suddenly, my father cut the motor. "Look", he said. My eyes followed the way he was pointing with his chin. There stood a magnificent creature, brown and sleek with long spindly legs that looked too small for its body. A large bull moose with an exceedingly huge rack of antlers was standing in the bulrushes chewing its cud. It looked at us, disinterested as we drifted by maybe 15 feet from it. I was in awe. This creature was so silent, it was so tall and it was so uninterested in our passing. As we drifted through the reeds again, my father restarted the motor. I turned to say, "That was great, Dad." My father smiled and nodded knowingly.

The rest of the morning passed uneventfully. We posted our signs as high on the trees as possible. One time my dad had to hold me up in the air and I had to post the sign, using the hammer and everything. It was a little crooked, but Dad seemed pleased. I looked for our moose as we left Lake St. John that day, but I never saw him.

There came a time the next fall when I was again told to get packed for a Lake St. John trip. Although the week had been warm, I was told to dress in long sleeves and a jacket. The mosquitoes would be hungry and the water would be colder. There was a possibility of rain. My job once again was to carry the nails in my pockets and the "No Trespassing" signs as best I could. Again, mom had a nice lunch packed in a brown paper bag from the butchers for us. I could smell the egg salad, my favourite. Another day to spend with my dad. Another chance to maybe see our moose.

We wove our way across the same route as before. The water was lower, so my job of watching for rocks was even more important. I was hoping and hoping that we would come to the same spot in the reeds and see that same moose, maybe even bigger than the last time.

But, again, as my father wove his way through the reeds, with only the sound of an occasional bird to accompany us, it was so still. Beer bottles in the water here and there, but no moose.

My mother had the foresight to send me to Lake St. John with rubber boots on that day, the black ones with the orange stripe around the top. As we neared the shore, drifting in, my father said, "Be careful. It's rocky", like he always did. I jumped in, now expertly, taking the rope with me to tie the boat up. My father unloaded his Dad stuff, including our lunch, while I checked my pockets for the twelve nails I had been given to look after. I still had the signs. They were mostly dry. "No Trespassing. This is an Indian Reserve."

Since there was no clear path, my job was to follow my father. "Stay close", he always said. I never knew why. I wasn't going anywhere. He knew how to work the motor and he was my ride home. Even though it was September, it was one of those final humid days. We needed rain. It would help the leaves change to their autumn colours.

    I dutifully followed my father, sweat beading on my brow under my Tilley-like hat. I had the nails all in my left jeans pocket. The signs, mounted on wood this time, were under my right arm. Walk, walk and watch for holes and rocks. I heard the swish, swish of my father's pant legs as walked through the tall grass. Stay close. It didn't seem like we were in far enough to put up the signs yet, when my father stopped dead in his tracks, without warning. I literally ran into him. He dropped his tools and the lunch he was carrying and stood stock still.

    Confused, I said, "Dad?" I stepped out to the left of him to see what had made him stop. What I saw was almost indistinguishable from the tall grass, now turning brown in those early fall days. It was browner and rounder than the grass and took up considerable space to my 9-year old way of thinking. My father walked slowly forward, with me closely following. As we got closer, I had a hard time initially figuring out what it was. It kind of reminded me of Granny's fur coat. But then I saw it had legs, long skinny ones. It was our moose.

    I had a rush of strange emotions. I was afraid and confused. I had an overwhelming feeling of sadness. I felt sick.

    My father veered to the right and crouched down at what should have been the head. But there was no head. It was gone. I watched in disbelief as my father ran his hand across the chopped-up flesh at the base of the neck where the head should have been. I realized then that a sickening smell hung in the air, the smell of rotting flesh. And I noticed the flies, all kinds of them buzzing around our moose. My father waved them away, but they continued to settle back down in clouds.

    Almost inaudibly, my father said only one word, "Chainsaw."

    It was the only time I ever saw my father cry.

    I thought I should do something, anything. So I put my little hand on his right shoulder as he knelt there. He suddenly stood up, wiped his eyes and reached into his inside breast pocket of his old checkered jacket. He retrieved a small flat tin and removed the lid. It contained tobacco. He looked at me and said, "Sherry Lynn, your Nookomis probably already taught you this. That's why we always travel with a little bit of tobacco. Tobacco was the first medicine given to our people in the beginning. It is offered as a gift at certain times. I offer it here now to this moose and to the Creator for the life that was this moose. I'll say a prayer to help this animal on its way. We'll give thanks for all that we have." He sprinkled the loose tobacco all over the moose carcass as he walked in a circle, holding my hand, clockwise. Then he raised his head skyward and began to pray. "Chi miigwech, Mnido." Thank you, Great Spirit. I only understood those first two words. The rest of the prayer was in Ojibway in the Mnjikaning dialect. I knew the Creator understood him. He kneeled once more when the prayer was done.

And then we went to work. He sent me back to our aluminum boat to retrieve the other bag of tools and a rope and both bailing buckets.

We spent the rest of the day in that clearing digging a hole with our bailing buckets big enough to put the moose in. I know now that it was a pulley my father rigged to the closest tree to move the large carcass into the hole we had made. It was hard, hot work. I was sent to retrieve rocks from the shoreline many times. We placed them on top of the grave when the job was done. The large moose, missing its head, was properly buried by the time we left Lake St. John that day. I always wondered if it was our moose. I couldn't be sure, because it was missing its head.

It was hot, it was smelly and my head was sweaty. We never did take a break to eat our egg-salad sandwiches. We did empty the whole thermos of its cool water, though.

Our original mission forgotten, we headed back across the lake to the west very close to suppertime. Mercifully, the rain held off. The nails were still in my jeans pocket and the signs were safely stowed in the bow of the boat. We stopped on the way home in the car to visit Granny. My Granny was glad to see me, as usual. She made me cocoa as she and my father spoke in Ojibway.

All these years later, I think lovingly about my father. Although long gone on to the spirit world, he had taken the time to instill a love of the land in me, a reverence for all of life around me. In those few hours on that fateful day, with little being said, he taught me vital life lessons about respect and honour.

There were many more trips to Lake St. John, but none as life altering as this one. Every fall, I continue to look forward to the day when I can take my grandchildren to Lake St. John, to show him the land his great grandfather owned. Today, it's still undeveloped, just the way my father left it. There's lot of room for deer, birds, foxes, rabbits, turtles and, yes, even a moose or two. Even though years have passed since my beloved trips with my father to Lake St. John, I know now what a special gift they were. My father, a simple man, was able to pass on lessons about what was important, not just for the present, but the future as well.

A gift to treasure.

Sherry and her son Jordan

The Winter of 1981

    I always wanted another girl. It was already fun dressing up my only daughter. I thought I should have a second girl, so I could dress her the same way: pink with lace and ruffles, cute little shoes, miniature purses and hair in a perfect little fountain on top of her head.

    Six months pregnant turned into seven, then eight in that winter of 1980. Finally, the time had come. Nine months and one day, two days... finally, seven days. I went into labour at 2:00 p.m. on March 12, 1981. In those days, ultrasounds were rare. They were only ordered if you were over 40 and might have one of those mongoloid babies.

    But, in fact, I was a rare expectant mother in my 20s who had an ultrasound. I didn't want to know if I was having a boy or a girl, so they never told me. I had that special test because I was so sick. Nauseous. Barfy. Dizzy. Not just up until week 12, but into months six and seven, all the way into month nine. I felt sick in the morning; I barfed morning, noon and night. Nothing I ate stayed down. The smell of coffee made the room spin. The aroma of eggs cooking made me retch.

    I was working at Georgian College then. Everyone knew how sick I was. My supervisor was so sympathetic I even had an extra 10 minutes added to my half hour lunch for barfing. So considerate. I loved that boss.

    I was sent for an ultrasound because I was so pregnant. They thought I was having twins. I was so big people figured I was overdue or having twins. Strangers would stop me to say "Ah, twins. Isn't that lovely?" I couldn't even fit into the booths at the Golden Dragon in downtown Orillia. I was huge. At any rate, the ultrasound said I was only having one baby. Not twins, even though my mother had a set, as did my grandmother's sister and my great aunt, too. I hoped it would be a girl. I resorted, at my obstetrician's urging, to try various kinds of food and drink to see what would stay down. It seemed that apple juice and dry crackers worked. But only if I had the meal before I got out of bed. I was put on a liquid super multi-vitamin regimen.

At one point, I had to go to the hospital once a week for intravenous food. I was hungry all the time. It was a total drag. I looked forward to getting rid of this baby and dressing her in pink.

So, the appointed hour came. Soon, I would be done barfing. Dr. R. Johnston, the only obstetrician in Orillia at the time, wasn't sure he would be able to stay to the very end. He was leaving for Florida and had to leave Orillia by 6:30 to catch his plane. We were all surprised when my labour progressed quickly. What began at 2:00 p.m., ended at 6:02 p.m., when my son was born. I remember exactly what Dick Johnston said "It's a boy, a big boy. Gotta go. He'll be 10 pounds easy." The experienced baby doctor was wrong. My new baby weighed 10 pounds, 15_ ounces.

His body was warm, the nurses told me, but his hands and feet were cold. He cried heartily and nursed hungrily. He was kept in an incubator. In those days, the hospital stays after birth were, on average, five days. They took my blood pressure a lot. They fed me well. I weighed six pounds less when I left the hospital than I did before I got pregnant. I had gained no weight during the pregnancy. I had actually lost six pounds.

It turns out my son wasn't just heavy, he was long – 25 inches long. No wonder I couldn't keep anything down. He took up so much space, there was no room left for my stomach or for food.

He had fat cheeks, big hands and feet and a cone-shaped head. The nurses assured me his head would eventually smooth out and look round. They were right.

My son was a famous baby in Soldiers' maternity ward. He didn't fit newborn or six-month baby clothes. Nurses wrapped him up in a blanket and he only wore his diaper. He was such a big lump of a baby, it was pretty easy to maneuver him. When you changed him, he just lay there like a blob. When you bathed him, he didn't move. He wasn't tiny and slippery like newborns. It was like bathing a three-month old. So, in those olden days in the early 80s, the nurses taught you how to do stuff: how to change a baby, bathe him and nurse him.

Since my baby was so compliant, he was the maternity ward demonstrator baby. All the other new moms got to practise being a new mom on my baby. He always came to me with a dry bum. And he smelled so good. I asked the nurse why. She told me because he got bathed three or four times a day. All the other mothers got to practise their diapering and bathing techniques on my son. His little head with his fluffy hair always smelled so fresh. I sighed with happiness.

My son's father and I wanted to give him a good name, so we called our baby Jordan. His middle name, Scott, comes from his grandfather on his father's side. I thought it sounded like a good name – Jordan Scott.

But the nurses didn't agree. I told them his name was Jordan Scott and that I wanted it printed on his little bassinette. The first nurse said, "You must be a big fan. Have you been on maternity leave long or have you always watched it?"

I thought I must have missed something. What was she talking about? Then another nurse came in. "She wants to call the baby Jordan Scott. Isn't that funny?" They both laughed.

"What are you talking about?" I finally asked, since no new information was forthcoming.

"Jordan Scott!" Nurse one responded. "You know, Jordan Scott, the bad guy from the soap. Which one is it? Y&R??" she asked Nurse two. She wasn't sure. But they both knew that Jordan Scott had recently been killed off on the afternoon soap opera.

Oh great, this new mom thought. Timing is everything.

Nurse number two printed my son's name in capital letters on the little roll-around bed. I could just imagine what people would think. "Jordan Scott, bad guy soap star, killed off, 1980." I thought for a moment of changing his name, but I didn't. It was a good name. If other people knew the same thing about my new son, they either quickly forgot or were too polite to mention it.

I took my son home to his sister, eighteen months his senior. He grew up to be a good-natured, active boy who always wanted to be the dog when he played house with his sister (I never asked). He has been a hockey player, lacrosse forward and football tight-end. He has grown up to be a big man, 300 pounds, 6 feet three inches and size 15 feet. His head hits the front-hall light fixture every time he visits. He can bench press 350 pounds. He cooks a mean chili and he is a wonderful father to his son, Paxton, my only grandchild.

I was never able to dress Jordan in pink lace or style his hair in the shape of a fountain coming out of the top of his head. But he is kind and capable and a hard worker and I love him.

Even though I am in my 50th year, I may yet get my chance to have another girl. My 28-year old daughter, who married in August, 2006, is three months pregnant. Timing is everything.

Bride-to-be Shannon and Jordan, Sherry's son

My Trip To Town

My mother was a nurse. I remember her always working. Most Christmas days, she wasn't there. Often, my Granny came to cook the turkey and my mother would, amazingly, be home to help eat it after dark.

It took me many years to realize that my mother was an alcoholic. I simply thought that everyone's mother drank. She worked. She came home and drank. Often, she fell asleep in the middle of the day. Years of therapy have taught me that she did the best with what she had. When she was dry, it didn't last for too long.

If my mother, as a parent, had to make do, then my little sister and I had to make do as the children of an alcoholic.

I remember I was, perhaps, in Grade 3. It was late summer and time to buy school clothes. I needed new shoes. My mother never learned to drive, which, in hindsight, was probably a good thing. She took a day off so that she could hire a driver and take us to town to buy me new school clothes. I had been poring over the Simpson's catalogue and knew I wanted a navy velvet jumper and a white blouse with ruffles, white leotards and new black shoes. I remember well that it was a Saturday.

It was a big deal for my mother to ask for and be given a Saturday off work. My mom got off her shift late, maybe 10:00 p.m. that Friday night. I waited for her so we could plan where we would go the next day and who would be driving us. I waited and waited until I fell asleep on the couch with the light and the TV on. She never came home. But she did arrive early the next morning. She had bleary eyes, her nurse's uniform was rumpled and her hair was not properly combed. She stopped to kiss me and cover me up and called me "sweetie pie." She then went straight to bed.

I awoke, sat up and rubbed my eyes, thinking it was a dream. But, no, she was asleep in her bed with her clothes on, snoring softly. But we were supposed to go to town today. I pushed her, I pulled her and I tried to wake her up. She was out cold. But I had to get my clothes for school. I had it all planned. We were supposed to go together.

In thinking about it, I have no idea where the rest of the family was that day: father, older brother and sister, younger sister. Maybe they had gone to visit relatives. I don't know and I've thought about it a lot since then.

Since it was early and it was a nice day, I decided that the bus going into town would be coming soon. I didn't know exactly what time it was supposed to come. I only knew that it came early before most people started work. I know now the Rama Rocket went by on its way to town at 8:10 a.m. It was much earlier than that. I washed my face, patted down my braids with some water and brushed my teeth like my mother had taught me. I found her black purse, the one with all the big zippers and dug out my mother's wallet. I took two twenties and all the change she had. I figured that should be enough. I went to the road to wait for the bus. The good thing about the Rama Rocket was that you had two chances to catch it. The first time it went past the house, it would go to the Longford store about a half mile to the north, turn around, wait a few minutes and come back again. I had no watch and didn't know what time it was. This was in the days before digital clocks were everywhere, including on the microwave. We didn't have a microwave.

So, I sat on the grass at the side of our long driveway and waited for the bus. Once a truck was coming down the road from town way and it looked like the bus. But when it got closer, I saw it was a truck and not the bus. Disappointment! But, eventually, the bus did come. My mother always told me to be extra careful crossing the Rama Road. Several kids from the reserve had been killed that she could remember and she always reminded me of that. So, I waited until the bus went past, heading north to the Longford store. I waved like a mad fool at the driver. He waved back.

A few minutes later, after I picked grass and burrs off me, the bus arrived and groaned to a halt right beside where I stood. The driver was cheery. "Where ya goin'?" he asked. "To town", I replied.

I dropped my quarter into the metal and glass box beside the driver and walked all the way to the back to find the very last seat on the right. That was normally where all the cool kids sat. But I was alone that day, until we got to the four corners where Rama Road, or County Road 44, meets the one road that goes due west to Victoria Park, and the opposite side road goes due east to the dump. That's where Mrs. Ingersoll with her brown paper bag that had carrying handles got on. She always wore a kerchief and didn't see me. I was kind of short in the back seat. One other person I didn't know got on at Sucker Creek. We all went into town.

I thanked the driver as I got off the bus, like my mother taught me to do. With my money carefully tucked away in my shorts pocket, I headed off to the shoe store across from the Opera House. I was too early. It wasn't open yet. So, I hung around, looking in the window. I could see they had my shoes.

I strolled down the street to the clothing store just past the Golden Dragon, but not on the same side. They had large rolls of material in the window. I couldn't tell if they had the jumper and blouse that I was after.

I walked up and down the street, watched the pigeons coo-coo. Finally, the shoe store opened. I was their first customer. And they did have the black shoes I needed and in my size, too. I walked around with them on in the store. They didn't quite go with my t-shirt and beige shorts and I wore no socks that day in my sneakers, but they seemed to fit fine. I paid for them with a twenty and was given lots of change in return. There was lots of money left to get my outfit.

Next, I entered Maude Arnem's Store and a saleslady with very red lipstick and her hair piled on her head stopped me at the door. "May I help you?" I told her what I came for. "Are you alone?" she asked, one eyebrow raised. "Yes, but I have money." She sniffed and took me to the back where outfits in my size were kept.

It turns out they didn't have a navy velvet jumper like the one in the Simpson's catalogue. However, she showed me a lovely plaid one – mostly green, with some navy and yellow and a white mock-necked blouse. I was encouraged to try them on in the little change room with the hook on the door. The saleslady seemed pleased that they fit so well. It would have to do. I almost forgot, but at the last minute, I asked her about white leotards. They were kept in large pull-out wooden drawers. She chose a package, looked me up and down and assured me they would fit. This purchase took all the rest of my money, but she did give me back some change.

I thanked the saleslady, who seemed nice now, as she handed me my brown paper sack with handles that had my clothes wrapped in tissue paper inside. I carried the other bag with my shoes in my other hand. I got outside into the bright sunlight and checked my money. I had two quarters, a dime, a couple of nickels and a bunch of pennies. I took one of the quarters and placed it carefully in the right-hand pocket of my shorts. That was money with which to catch the lunchtime bus back home.

I was hungry by now and really wanted some French fries from the Golden Dragon. I went in and took a booth near the front. Ting came to serve me and said in her heavy Chinese accent, "You alone, girl?" I said, "yes", but told her I had money. I pulled it out of my pocket and laid it on the table, except for my quarter for the bus. She tsk-tsked and shook her head. "What you want?"

I told her I wanted French fries please with gravy. "Gravy, too?" she said in disbelief. She walked back toward he kitchen shaking her head. A few minutes later, she brought me fries and gravy on a smaller plate than usual. I quickly gobbled them up. She also brought me a glass of ice-cold water. More and more people started to come into the restaurant as Ting took my money at the checkout near the door.

Maneuvering my two bags around the heavy doors, I thought it must almost be time to catch the lunchtime bus home. I waited for what seemed like a long time. But, eventually, the bus did come and as I paid my quarter, the driver smiled at me. I made my way with my two shopping bags to the rear of the bus, into my cool seat. No one else got on the bus with me for the ride home. I decided to get off the bus on the opposite side of the road from my driveway, like a big girl. The driver warned me to be careful crossing the road.

I made it safely across the road and ran down the driveway to show my mom my new school clothes and shoes. The door was unlocked like it always was, but there was no one home. My mother was gone. To work, I figured.

I was tired. It had been a pretty busy day. I tried on my clothes – mock-necked white top, plaid jumper, white leotards and black shoes. All fit perfectly. I admired myself, turning this way and that in the full-length mirror mounted on the back of the bedroom door. I was a big girl, a clever girl to go shopping by myself. I would have lots of new friends admire my clothes on the first day of school.

I took off my new clothes and hung them up carefully in the closet I shared with my sisters, with the black shoes underneath. I lay down in my bed for a little sleep. When I awoke, my father was home and he had brought people with him. They were noisily playing cards in the kitchen.

I don't remember if my mother returned home that night. I only know I was too tired to wait for her again. We never spoke of my trip into town. Ever.

In a childhood spent with an alcoholic, days turn into weeks that turn into hazy months. You do what you have to do to get by.

My mother died in her 42nd year when I was eighteen. I still miss her and now belong to that select group of women known as "motherless daughters." I'm sure she did the best she could.

And I vowed I would do better.

Firewood

It was one of those snapping cold, yet clear, late winter days. Granny had let me sleep in and I was snuggled safely in her big brass bed with the feather duvet on top, the one with the white lace where your neck goes. I knew it was cold because I could see those miniature snowflakes that had formed on the inside of the old rattling windows that faced north. I knew Granny would be making porridge for me because she loved me.

"Sherry Lynn! Sherry Lynn!" I hear Granny calling from downstairs. "Time to get up."

I know if I ignore her that will buy me a few more minutes in this warm toasty bed. I see the sun shining through the frosted window, but know it will still be cold when my feet hit the wooden floor.

Finally, tired of calling, Granny comes upstairs. "You lazy thing, time to get up. Look, I brought my extra moccasins for you to wear. Hurry now, I need you to get some firewood."

I swing my feet out of the comfortable bed and am pleasantly surprised when my feet notice that the moccasins are already warm. I smile at my Gran, convinced she loves me, because she has warmed them up in front of the old woodstove. Just for me. Gran smiles back. She's holding one of her old shawls, the green one.

"Quick, put this on." It's way too big, but has very few holes. "It'll keep you warm while you run out quickly to the woodpile. Come on, come on."

I groan inwardly as I follow Gran down the old wooden staircase, the one with a strip of rug down the middle. It is cold. And I'm thinking I'll run quickly out to the woodshed and get back in as fast as possible.

Granny adds, "Go quick. Your porridge is ready." I can smell the maple syrup she has warming in a little pan on the stove. And the kitchen is warm and I can smell the wood smoke.

Granny opens the door and holds the screen for me. "Carry as much as you can, so you only have to go once. Hurry."

And in my 9-year old mind, I'm thinking to myself, it's not worth it. I have to freeze all the way out and all the way back and for what? Porridge? But Granny is old, my father always reminded me. Be good.

So I run quickly down those few rickety steps and past the old clothesline and on to the woodshed. The path through the little bit of snow we had that year is well worn. The moccasins are too big, but they are warm. And the shawl, knotted at my neck, does help a lot. Get to the shed, yank open the door, stare into the dark. And Granny urges me on, holding open the screen door and looking to the east. "Come on, quick."

And I step into that woodshed and I guess it's not as cold as I thought it was going to be. And I pile up three pieces, no four, if I stack them the way Granny taught me on my bent arms, I can even carry six. And I hurry back towards the house.

I get to the foot of the steps and remember I never closed the shed door and I look up at Granny for help. And she says, "Never mind the door, I'll get it after."

And I realize my breathing is laboured and I'm sweating.

Run up those rickety steps, three, four, five, to Granny, who is holding the door for me.

I try to squeeze by, but Granny stops me. "Do you hear it?" she asks.

And I think, hear what? My heart beating? My fast breathing? Those little drops of sweat rolling off my head and hitting the porch?

"Do you heart it?" Gran asks again. "Listen."

And I try to squeeze by her with my wood. It's cold you know.

She says, "Stop. Listen. Do you hear it?"

And I'm confused and cold and say, "Please, Gran. I'm cold."

"I know. I know. Listen." She turns me to the east, the way she is facing.

And I listen really hard and my breathing slows a bit. And it's quiet and it's crisp and the sun is glistening off what little snow we got that year.

Then I hear it. The sound of a bird singing. Just one.

"I hear him, Gran."

"Ah, yes", my Gran declares. "He's singing for spring. It won't be long now. Come on, get in here. You'll catch your death of cold."

The screen door slams shut behind us and Gran pulls the old wooden door shut, the one with the ancient brass lock.

"O.K. Porridge is ready. And I warmed you up some maple syrup for it."

And as I sit in my chair and watch my Gran bustle about the kitchen, adding wood to the fire and serving me, I wonder why she didn't go out and get the wood herself. But I never ask. I think of what my father would say. "Be good. She's old, you know."

It was years later, when I came to understand the important lesson my beloved Granny shared with me that day.

And even now, no matter what I am doing, or how busy I am, I always take the time in those final cold crisp mornings of late winter, to listen for birdsong.

Sherry's mother hanging clothes at the "old house", note woodshed in background - circa 1950

Gramma and grandson Robert

Alberta Bound

In almost fifty years, I've spent only about two hours in total with Gramma, my husband's grandmother. I've decided she is an amazing woman.

Four years ago, Rob and I travelled to Eckville, Alberta to visit his elderly grandmother. She had broken her hip six months before and we wondered how many more years she might live. You see, in June 2006, Gramma turned ninety-seven.

Gramma lives in the Manor, a very modern, assisted-living facility. She has her own room with a lovely view of the garden outside her window. She eats her meals in a communal dining room. There are personal support workers on staff, a cook, housekeepers and a nurse in charge.

None of the residents of the Manor are bedridden. They all need to be independent. It seems that everyone who lives there uses either a cane or a walker, mostly walkers.

We were going to Jasper, Alberta because I had to speak at a national tourism conference in late October. We flew to Edmonton from Toronto, drove to Jasper and then drove through the Rockies to the Red Deer area. It was very good weather. The mountains were magnificent. Photos don't really do them justice.

We arrived at Auntie Marion's (the sister of my husband's father) and planned to stay a few days. We definitely planned to visit Gramma, about a half hour's drive away.

Auntie Marion is the historian in the family, obsessively clipping newspapers and carefully writing on the back of every photo she takes: the person's name, date, place and event. One photo shows a much younger smiling Gramma. It says in Auntie Marion's stilted script "Mom (Gramma) 85th birthday at John and Sue's, near Red Deer (June 1994)." Gramma is impeccably dressed as usual. White blouse, navy sweater, navy checked skirt, black sensible shoes. And her string of pearls, always the pearls. More recently, she has taken to wearing a little pearl angel pin.

Gramma is much shorter than she used to be. She walks only with her walker now. Aunt Marion visits her at least once a week, maybe more. She checks to make sure Gramma is taking her pills – one each day for blood pressure (just a little high) and others that are just plain vitamins: calcium, vitamin B and vitamin D. I take more pills than Gramma does.

Gramma is quite deaf and wears two hearing aids. I don't know how well they work on her 97-year old ears, though. But if you speak to her face to face and there is little or no background noise, she hears almost fine.

During our four-hour plane ride, I wondered how Gramma would be now, a full 52 months after our last visit. Would she be feeble, more forgetful, blind, even more deaf? Would she know us? I wondered how many more times we would meet. This will probably be the last time we see her, I think to myself. Then, again, we thought the last time would be the last.

Auntie Marion must have briefed her mother. We walk into the Manor, sign the guest book and head towards her room. But, Gramma was at her usual dining spot at her table, waiting for us instead. Marion spoke to Gramma first, "Mom, you have visitors."

Gramma turns our way. "Hello, dear. It's so nice to see you." She just beamed. She planted a wet kiss on both of our cheeks and squeezed our hands. She looked exactly the same as she always had.

Gramma was wearing a pink ruffle-necked sweater (this time, no pearls), black pants and the same sensible shoes. What – pants? What happened to the skirt she always wore? On the way to Gramma's room, I whisper to Auntie Marion, "Why is she wearing pants?" I learned later that up until this past July, Gramma had always worn a skirt with pantyhose, always. Even with her hunched-over little body, she put pantyhose on every day. Even with her arthritic little wrinkled hands, she puts pantyhose on every day. Auntie Marion explained that Gramma had to lay on her back on her single bed with her feet in the air to put the pantyhose on carefully and slowly one leg at a time. Sometimes it could take her up to an hour. And they were never even wrinkled, no backward toes, no baggy ankles. They were perfectly straight and smooth. Gramma told Auntie Marion one time that ladies always wear pantyhose. I don't even wear pantyhose – too much work. Guess Gramma figured it was time to finally slack off a little this summer and wear socks and pants instead.

We learned during this trip how Gramma ended up in Alberta with four of her five children. It turns out her first husband was a philanderer, those are Gramma's exact words "philanderer." It's not a word you hear much anymore, but it's a word that doesn't have several meanings. You know right away what the word is trying to say. But I digress.

Gramma left Coldwater in the middle of the night and took two of her three young children with her. She left one with his grandparents. She said she'd come back for him, but she never did. But that is another story.

So she left with one boy and one girl (Auntie Marion) and she was five months' pregnant with Auntie Faith, the second youngest. In the middle of the night, with little money, no training or education, she left to make a new life for herself and her children and her new man in the 1930s. She must have been afraid, but one thing I'm sure of, Gramma had to be brave. Altogether, Gramma had three husbands. She outlived them all, even the philanderer.

She has lived in Coldwater, Michigan and Alberta. It looks like she will live out her life in Eckville.

Gramma smiles easily. She has white hair and blue eyes and wears enormous eye glasses. She calls everyone "dear" and has a positive outlook on life.

She never complains about anything, never a negative word about her life or her health. I will never forget one of the last conversations I had with Gramma. "How do you feel, Gramma?" I asked her. "Do you have pain anywhere?" She looked perplexed. I repeated my question. She answered, "No, dear. I feel fine. I don't hurt anywhere. I feel good. I'm very lucky. You know, dear, I watch some of the old people who live here. They walk slow. They moan and groan every time they sit down or get up. They talk about all the pills they take. The poor old souls. I sometimes feel sorry for them. So, did you come from Ontario by train?"

Sometimes people in their 90s switch topics quickly without warning. You have to keep up. Imagine Gramma worrying about the old people who live at the Manor. She doesn't know she's an old person, too.

Our trip to Alberta was good for my soul in more ways than one. I wonder how I will act when I'm old. Will I wear pantyhose? Will I worry about other old people? Will I wear pearls?

I think about our next trip out West, probably in four years. Gramma will be 101 by that time. I treasure the two photos Auntie Marion sent home with us. "Gramma going for lunch in Marion's van (Eckville – Fall 2006)." And "Gramma and grandson, Rob, at the Manor (Eckville – October, 2006)." Gramma is smiling in both of them.

I've decided that Gramma is a remarkable woman! Each of us would do well to have half her strength and kindness.

Chief Douglas, far right, at yet another meeting

Band Council Meeting In The Old Hall

Stories my paternal Grandmother told me about those days before I was born continue to rattle around in my head lately. Nookomis spoke of solstice ceremonies, of setting snares for rabbits in winter, of walking to the natural spring to fetch water every day. She passed these stories on to her only son, my father, who passed them on to me. But the following story was not passed on to me in hushed tones. It really happened. I was there.

My father, Irvin Douglas, was Chief of the Chippewas of Rama for nearly two decades. I remember clearly as I was growing up, all the battles he waged with the Indian Agent and the government of the time. He wrote letters, he attended meetings. It was only when I was much older that I understood what that word "Government" meant, always written with a capital G.

One day in the springtime when I was eight or nine years old, my father told me he was taking me to a council meeting that night. They were always held in the evening in those days. I recall my mother telling my dad that I shouldn't go. It would be too late on a school night by the time the meeting was over. School was important. My father was adamant.

"Peggy. Think of what Sherry Lynn might learn in those few hours," my father said. "She should go."

My mother gave in. My father was right.

Council meetings in those days took place in the old community hall, long since then condemned by the government as an unsafe building. In the 1980s, a new council chamber and band office were constructed with dedicated space for meetings with government officials. But, for many, many years, those council meetings took place in the old hall.

So I went to the council meeting with my father, the Chief. Before we arrived, he told me I had to sit quietly and listen. In those days, any member of the public could come and speak to the council and ask for their help on various issues. They always spoke first, before the regular band business was conducted. I was in awe of the Indian Agent, who, it seemed, was there to run the meeting. He wore a brown three-piece suit, smoked cigars and spoke loudly to keep people's attention. He sat beside my father at the meeting. Before we started, there was coffee and tea made and everyone helped themselves to a cup. All the councillors made sure to come and speak to me, several of them in Ojibway. They seemed pleased that I was there.

The first community member that evening to speak was one of the elders. She talked about five minutes, partly in English and partly in Ojibway. With my limited knowledge of the Mnjikaning dialect, I knew she was talking about some issue with her drinking water. She had health problems. She was getting on in years. My father and the councillors nodded in agreement. The Indian Agent seemed displeased. My father stood up to shake her hand and he began to respond to her concerns in Ojibway.

The Indian Agent raised his hand. "Irvin, er, Chief..." he began. "As you know, I only speak English. This council meeting is only to be conducted in Her Majesty's English language."

My father, the Chief, always kind, gave a look to the Indian Agent that was difficult for my young mind to decipher. There was some murmuring in Ojibway around the council chamber. Whispering. My father said something in Ojibway to his council. One by one, going clockwise around the circle, they each nodded in the affirmative. My father said something in Ojibway to the elder who had come to speak to council and she headed to the door. Council stood up all at the same time.

I remember the seven words very clearly that my father, the Chief, directed at the Indian Agent who sat beside him that night. "We have agreed this meeting is over."

Chairs were pushed back and my father came to get me. We left.

I looked over my shoulder as I exited the main doors of the old meeting hall that night and I thought to myself that my mother would be so happy that I was home early. I will never forget the look of anger on the face of the Indian Agent. His cigar was firmly clenched in the corner of his mouth.

It turned out that we didn't go home alone that night. As my mother tucked me into bed, a vehicle arrived with several of the councillors. Councillor Simcoe rode his bike to our house.

I know my mother made tea because I could hear the kettle whistle. And, long into the night, I could hear the councillors and their Chief speak about important issues in their mother tongue. I expect that no minutes were taken of that meeting. But, I'm sure they dealt with business vital to our little community.

As I grew up, I heard many more stories about Government interference in our lives: the days when we needed a pass signed by the Indian Agent to go into town to the grocery store, the day the last treaties were signed, the time they came to take our children to the residential school.

As the years went by, I came to understand that throughout history, the Government did not just exert influence over our community, but they had a say in our families and even controlled, at times, what was in our heads and our hearts.

I am grateful that my father deemed it important enough to show his children all the faces of local politics. I believe it has made me and my siblings behave in a certain way as adults and we understood things in a different way from most people. I was the youngest elected councillor in the history of our community, at the age of 21. Although long gone on to the Spirit World, I believe our parents would be pleased with how we turned out.

Chi miigwech, Dad, for taking me to my first band council meeting in the old hall so long ago.

David H. Church Primary class, Sherry 4th from right, top row, circa 1960's

School Pictures

My grandmother, my father's mother (in our language, my Nookomis) was a constant positive force in my life. She was my main babysitter as I was growing up. She was a great cook. She taught me so many things, lessons that a young Ojibway woman would need throughout her lifetime.

She lived just two miles from my childhood home and as soon as I was able, I often rode my purple bicycle with the banana seat to my beloved Granny's every chance I got. In the winter, if there were someone going to town, I would hitch a ride and drop in unexpectedly. But more often than not, I walked the short two miles and couldn't wait to be wrapped in Granny's loving arms.

Time went on, as it does for all of us. In later years, Granny's health began to deteriorate. She suffered from congestive heart failure and "just a touch of arthritis", according to her. She walked every day. She often opened a window for fresh air, even in the winter. She preached moderation in all things.

I would sit at her feet on the hooked rug just in front of her rocking chair for hours on end, listening to stories of the old days. She tried very hard to teach me to make porcupine quill baskets, but I did not have the fine motor skills or the patience. She sang old church songs in English. She taught me Ojibway. She was a kind woman whom I adored.

As I grew up and got married, I was pleased to see how my children first observed their great grandmother with a kind of quiet curiosity. She was getting older, a little frail. My daughter, now 27, can still recall Granny's fascinating ancient hands. You could see through the thin dark skin. Her arthritis had thickened her joints. Her skin was so soft and smooth and you could clearly see the veins in her hands. Her hands had put in a lifetime of hard work, washing floors, doing laundry, cooking meals and making those wonderful baskets. She worked for many years doing "day work", cleaning the houses of the old moneyed Orillians. My older son had a special relationship with my Granny. He was always glad to see her. He would burst out of my car and run to his Gran, slamming the old wooden screen door behind him. She would sweep his short sturdy body up, plant a kiss on his little head and settle into her old creaky rocking chair with a story for "her boy" as she called him.

And there were always cookies at Gran's house. An old blue transferware biscuit jar sat on her kitchen counter, always full to the brim with cookies. All the children of the neighbourhood called my Gran "granny". She was a grandmother to them all.

Time marched on. Granny was in and out of nursing homes. She couldn't live somewhere else while her house was just sitting there empty. It just made sense for us to leave her in her home as long as possible. In between trips to the hospital and home nursing care, we tried not to talk about "assisted living".

My three children were used to my taking them to see Granny. She would always make tea for me and lemonade for my children, no matter the season.

Every year I always ordered an extra set of school pictures of all three children for my Granny. She would proudly display them in her tiny well-kept living room. In the three frames she would not remove their older picture, the one from last year. She would just take the frame apart carefully and add the new photo to the front. This meant that one frame for each child held their school photos from kindergarten onwards. I figured when all of them got to high school that Granny would have to get three new frames, because no way could another four years of photos fit into them.

It so happened it was the fall of the year, again the time for school pictures. I made sure, as any good mother would do, that all three were dressed in their finest on picture day. Their hair was nicely combed. My daughter wore only matching hair accessories. There were several family members who would display these photos proudly for a full year, my Granny included.

Even though money in those days was tight for me, with three children under the age of 12 and my husband working only part-time, I made sure to save enough in my budget for the school photos. I always ordered three 5 by 7s for Granny, since that was the size of her special frames.

The photos arrived in early winter that year. I separated them and wrote names and ages on the backs. They all looked pretty good. I sent my money in the envelope back to the home-room teachers. Now the photos were mine to give away.

I had dropped all three children at three different places that evening, one at hockey practice, one at music lessons and one at a friend's. It would give me about an hour of free time, enough time to visit Granny and take her the latest school pictures.

I pulled into Granny's driveway about 6:30 p.m. It was already dark. A light shone in her kitchen window as well as in her living room. "That's strange", I thought. Granny is never one to waste electricity. She couldn't know that I was coming. I grabbed the photos and got out of the car quickly since I'm on a time limit and as I'm heading to the step, I notice that her perennial flowers at the front door had not been cut back for the winter. Granny was always so particular about putting her flowers to bed for the winter.

On the porch in the brisk evening cold, I could hear the TV on, to a program I don't recognize as one of Granny's favourites. Photos in my hand, things aren't making sense.

I realize then that there are new curtains in the living room window – sheers actually. That's funny. I knock on the door. It opens quickly. But standing there is not my grandmother. It's Bernard, who works for public works. Two of his daughters peer out from behind him, wondering who has come to visit at this hour on a week night.

And then it hits me. Granny doesn't live here anymore. She died the spring before. It was a very large funeral. We have already split up her few belongings among us. My son has her rocking chair. I have the cookie jar.

Bernard says, "Hi" haltingly. I mumble an "I'm sorry", turn and leave Granny's porch with the photos still clutched to my chest. I get into the car and slam the door, tears streaming down my face. I throw the photos onto the passenger seat. I sob into my hands as they clasp the steering wheel tightly. I don't know how long I sat there, but eventually the porch light was turned off.

Very soon, it is time to pick up my three children in reverse order and take them home. I tuck them into bed and cast a glance at my Granny's rocking chair (now my son's) in the corner of the boy's bedroom. His little slippers are sitting casually in front of the chair.

My Granny is gone. She's not coming back. All I have is a treasure trove of memories and stories. And I decide then that I have to make sure my children hear those stories and, off in the future, that my grandchildren do as well.

The next day, I carefully wrap those three photos in plastic and deliver them to Granny's grave. Using tape and rocks, I attach them as best I can to her gravestone. And I know that she is as pleased as I am about how well they turned out.

Not everyone has loved someone so deeply that they have difficulty letting them go. I consider my deep abiding love for my Granny one of life's greatest gifts.

Years later, the Mnjikaning community began a search for a large enough piece of land, fully serviced, on the main road, on which to build a new and improved daycare. A deal was struck with my family.

Our state of the art, $2.6 million child-care centre, offering programs and services to families of new babies and toddlers alike, will open just after Hallowe'en this year. It is fitting that the exact place where so many children shared cookies with my grandmother will now, for all time, be a place of learning for young Ojibway children.

They will sing old songs in English. They will learn new ones in Ojibway. They will share meals and stories and tales of how it used to be.

I miss you, Gran, and I think of you every day.

You would be proud of what we have done with our lives and our community.

New Child Care Centre 2006, located on former site of "old house"

From Wartime To School Time

Each of us has a story of how we came to be where we are now. Mnjikaning has been here on the east side of Lake Couchiching for well over 150 years. Telling each of our stories individually and collectively adds up to an accurate history of our community. Mnjikaning has a long and honourable history, one that needs telling, especially during this time of great change.

I can only tell the story of the last 50 years firsthand. Other details have been given to me by family, historians and community members.

During the First and Second World Wars, many of our people signed up. Some did not come home. Those who did, carried disturbing memories of barbed wire, mustard gas and gunfire that lit up the night sky. Many were wounded. Upon returning, most of these Native veterans experienced ongoing problems with government bureaucracy: missed pension cheques, non-existent land grants (as promised), substandard medical care. These men and women, who had put their lives on the line, were poorly treated or ignored by a country who urged them to enlist.

In the Rama United Church is a yellowed "Honour Roll" of those who served, framed and hanging on the wall. Over a decade after the end of World War II, it finally became legal for Indians to consume alcohol. This meant that Native war veterans were able to go into the Royal Canadian Legion in Orillia for the first time in the 1960s. But there was another issue concerning Native war veterans outstanding. None of the local cenotaphs or memorials to veterans contain the names of any of our people – no Williams, no Andersons, no Shillings, no Stinsons, no Noganoshes or Snaches or Bensons or Douglases. Again, First Nations people have been passed over or left out.

A small but dedicated group of Rama veterans got together in the 1970s to right that wrong. The Rama Veterans Club fundraised and accepted donations so that a local war memorial could be erected. It was a proud early winter day in 1977 when those who had served once again put on their uniforms (if they still fit) or their Sunday best, polished and pinned on the medals they had been given and attended the unveiling of Rama's war memorial. The whole community turned out. The memorial stands immediately to the north of the Church. A star beside one's name denotes "deceased." Sadly, there are more and more stars added each year. It serves as an enduring reminder of the freedoms we enjoy today because of those who served. On Remembrance Day especially, the stone is not silent. The names of those etched upon it continue to say, "Lest We Forget."

For many years, there was no Band Office in Rama. The secretary/treasurer was housed at the old school, the brick building directly across from the church. Next to the church was the old community hall, a two-storey frame structure that would never pass a fire code inspection by today's standards.

The two-room schoolhouse had two classes and two teachers. The lower grades were together in the room to the north and another class from grade 5 up to grade 8 was on the south side. Miss Bellhouse was the lower grade teacher. She was young, pretty and fair-skinned. She got engaged the last year the Rama school was open, maybe in 1963. I believe she would have described her Native students as "shy." She taught us to stand up when spoken to. She found it confusing to have two 5-year old boys named Ted, so one had to be called Ted and the other had to be called Ed from that day forward. They still are.

In the entryway of the old school was the large rope hanging down from a hole in the ceiling to ring the bell. You were in deep trouble if you rang it. Speaking Indian could attract the same punishment. The leather strap was a common form of punishment at the hands of Madame Principal in those days. Upstairs at the back of the school lived the Kings.

When you reached high school age, there was no more school to attend on the reserve. My brother Mark and sister Sharon went to school in Orillia. The Rama School was closed in the 1960s. The Department of Indian Affairs as well as Ontario educators believed it best for all concerned that Indian children went to school with non-Indian children. We had to learn to "fit in".

We rode the big yellow bus into Orillia where reserve children attended David H. Church School and, later, Regent Park. I will never, ever forget my first day at David H. Public School.

My mother was a nurse and seemed to be gone most of my childhood. I knew she truly loved me, though, when she took a vacation day from work to make sure I got on the school bus safely for the first time.

It was a glorious fall day, with the sun shining and the maple leaves just starting to turn colour. I was dressed in my very best black velvet jumper, white blouse with ruffles at the cuffs, white leotards and black t-strap patent leather shoes. They were so shiny. If I held them close to my face, I was reflected in them. My mother had carefully braided my hair into two braids. She always wet my hair first, so as it dried, the braids would shrink even tighter.

Mom had supervised the brushing of my "beaver teeth", as she used to call them. She made sure I had an old striped tea towel in the neck of my jumper so I wouldn't mess up my new clothes as I put the toothpaste on my toothbrush.

Mom held my hand as we walked up our long driveway to wait for the school bus. She hummed, as she often did, as we walked. We stood well back from the road, all the while my mother warning me about the hazards of traffic. She hummed and rocked back and forth on her feet, front to back, all the while holding my hand.

Finally, we looked to the north on Rama Road and saw the big yellow school bus chugging our way. There was no one else on it yet. Ours was the first house. I was excited and nervous. I looked nice and clean. But would my teacher be mean to me? Would I get lost?

The bus stopped right in front of us and the red-haired driver looked our way. He looked friendly and said "hello".

I gripped Mom's hand tighter. My mother crouched down and turned my face to hers. "You'll be all right, Sherry Lynn. Try to stay clean. Good luck! I'll see you tonight. And, remember, try to act like them." She kissed me on the cheek.

Mom helped place me on the first step of the big bus with my right hand on the handrail.

I turned to protest, to talk more, to get more information. Before I knew it, I was up the steps, safely sitting on the front seat to the right of the driver. I looked out the window. My mother was smiling and waving. Her words rolled around in my head. "Try to act like them." What did she mean? Who were them?

After I got to David H., it didn't take me long to figure out who "them" were.

But that's another story.

Unveiling of cenotaph 1977, note old Community Centre in background

Chief Irvin Douglas unveiling memorial

Hands

As I look at my hands in my 50th year, I see my mother's square fingers, wrinkled knuckles, nails that swoop up, touch of arthritis. My mother got to use her hands for only 42 years. Well, her whole body. She died of an asthma attack. Back then, they didn't know what they know now.

My hands have had an interesting life, so far. My earliest memory is holding my mother's hand as she walked me to the end of the driveway to wait for the school bus on the first day of school. My mother's hand was warm and comforting. Fast forward some years after that. I can see bigger hands holding the smaller hand of my little sister. There are 2 years difference between us and I can hear my mother saying, "Now, Sherry Lynn, hold your little sister's hand." We're on our way to the Longford store. The instructions continue, "Walk facing traffic. Keep Sharla on the inside. And jump in the ditch when a car goes by." I mostly followed the rules, except for the "jump in the ditch" part.

I can see my hands on the handlebars, the first time I rode my bike alone. It was at the house of my father's distant cousin at Lake Scugog. Their last name was Edgar. One of the older kids, I don't remember his name, put me on his silver bicycle and pushed me down the hill. He said I was 8 and was going to learn to ride a bike that week-end, "by hook or by crook". I had the pedalling down pat, but I kept falling over. My knees had little stones in them from falling so often. My hands hurt from squeezing the black rubber handlebar grips so tight. That older boy was pushing me and kind of running along behind me, shouting encouragement. The other kids were shouting, too, no, cheering. They were calling my name. They were behind me, way, way behind me. And below my hands, I could see my legs pumping furiously. The sun was shining. I was going and going and going. But, no one had told me how to make a bike stop. So,

I just kept going until I quit pedalling and the bike slowed and slowed and finally stopped. My knees got more little stones in them when I fell off.

I can see my hands holding a fishing rod. My dad and I are in the old aluminum boat, the one with dents and dings in the front. We are in Geneva Park bay and there is no one else on Lake Couchiching. My hands hold the rod and my eyes watch the red and white bobber waiting for a muskellunge to take it. I hold the rod up in the air as I sit there. I never rest it on the side. That's lazy. I squint up at my dad, who doesn't need to sit down. He has a grey and black ball cap on. I think it used to be white and black, but now it's grey and black. It's old. A Player's™ cigarette hangs from the corner of his mouth, the smoke drifting lazily to the north. I watch his hands as he casts, effortlessly. His left hand moves in a fluid motion. When the lure hits the water, the casting rod snaps. His right hand winds up the line, slowly. I look at my hands, both on my fishing rod, still in exactly the same place. To be a fisherman, you need to have patience. I wait for my muskellunge.

Many years later, after my hands learn to write, I learn to type, too. For 15 years I work in libraries and my hands file hundreds and hundreds of index cars, alphabetically, of course, and there are rules to follow: nothing before something, treat 'mac' and 'mc' as if they're both 'mac'. My hands have handled lots and lots of paper, books, magazines, newspapers and so many index cards. And, sometimes, I stamped cards and even dusted shelves. I see my hands pushing an old oak book cart full of books. The cart could hold up to 150 books at a time. I know! I counted them with these very hands.

I can see my hands through the years resting on my stomach as my son's foot kicks so hard, you can see my hand move. I cradle my newborn baby. Years later, we plant seeds together in the window box. I shake the tiny seeds out of the paper seed packet into my right hand. I hold out his little hand, flat beneath mine. I cup my hand and turn it sideways and let the tiny seeds fall in a straight line into his. He places them carefully in the dirt. We water them together. Later, they bloom and my son is in awe, of the seeds and of his mother.

As the years go by, I see my hands braid my daughter's hair. Her hair is dark and thick and even when wet, hard to maneuver into the 3 parts necessary for a neat, tight braid. Rarely is it good enough the first time. I see my hands twist hand over hand until the braid is straight and falls squarely down her back. I tie the eagle fluff hair tie right at the top of the braid in the thickest part. There, perfect! I kiss her on the cheek, my hands on her shoulders and send her out to join the circle. My only daughter is a pow-wow dancer.

The years go by. There are good times and bad. Life ebbs and flows as it is meant to do. And, more recently, my hands once again remember how to soothe a fussy baby, how to change diapers, how to take liquid Tylenol™ out of a small bottle using a dropper and putting it right into the baby's mouth, so none of its stains his little blue sleeper. Now, my grandson is 15 months old. When I pick him up and he rests his sweet-smelling little head with the wispy hair right in the crook of my neck. His little hands reach under my arms and around to my back as he's snuggled there and Pax's little hands pat me on the back.

Before our last trip south, my mother-in-law had been told she had maybe three months left on this earth. I had a precious few minutes alone with Doreen. I crouched down and told her we didn't have to go on our trip. She clasped my hand in hers and said, "Don't be silly. If there's anything I've learned from being sick, it's live your life." I stare at my mother-in-law's hands holding mine and think how they don't look like mine at all. Her fingers are short and slender, her wrists are so thin you can see the veins through them. They are fragile and tired. I give her a quick peck on the cheek. A smile, a wave and then we're gone. It's the last time we spoke. "Live your life."

I see my hands hold tightly onto the bus seat ahead of me. We are winding up the side of a mountain after dark. Narrow road, hairpin turns. My ears pop. The driver has to gear up and gear down constantly. The road is so steep that, at times, we are pinned to our seats. Bags and knapsacks fall from the overhead bins. I think I am praying. The road signs aren't in English. I'm sure we're lost. People in the back of the bus are saying "I'm gonna be sick." We keep climbing. Finally, the bus lurches to a stop. We get out and retrieve our luggage. It's late and there is no elevator. Bus passengers fall into their beds and hope tomorrow will be better in the Swiss Alps.

The day breaks, cool and crisp. I don't sleep well, so I am the first one up, showered and dressed. I figure that way, this high up at least, I'll have hot water. I pull on my light jacket and tuck a scarf in at my throat for added warmth. The old outer door creaks as I open it and step outside. The sun is just coming up. In our dialect, it's "biidabun", when you see that very first light of the day. It is the cleanest air I have ever breathed. I stop at the edge. The mountains are magnificent. A town on the side of the mountain looks just like little specks of buildings huddled together. A light mist covers everything. And it is so quiet. I'm overwhelmed at the beauty and silence of this place and this moment. Even though I know I'm alone, I know I'm not. I am reminded of a line from a famous book and I say it aloud. "Be still and know that I am God." I remove my glasses with my hands and wipe tears from my eyes.

Weeks later, after I've delivered the eulogy for my mother-in-law, there isn't a dry eye in the house, mine included. I sigh heavily and take my seat in the special "Reserved for Family Section." My husband reaches for my free left hand. My right hand holds Kleenex™. He holds my hand open and with his left hand, spells something on my outstretched hand. He draws a heart and then a capital U. I…heart…you. No, no, I love you. He holds my left hand in his right. I lean into him and we sob together quietly as we say goodbye to his mother.

Our hands are something that are in front of us every day, yet we hardly ever look at them. But they have so many stories to tell. As time marches on, the veins in my hands show through more clearly. The knuckles are more wrinkled. My hands have wiped away tears, clapped in joy and waved goodbye. And they still have a whole lifetime of work ahead of them.

Passport photo of Sherry's mother

𝒯he ℒost 𝒦ey

    Rob told me I really needed to clean up my home office. There was so much stuff on top of the desk he bought me 12 years ago, that every time I added just one more envelope, piles of paper slid onto the floor. Even my office chair was covered with Christmas wrap, dollar store bags, MacDonald's Happy Meal™ toys.
    So, I took half a day and plowed through it. I'm such a packrat. I can't throw anything out that someone somewhere in Canada might need some day. Rob reminds me I'm not the National Library or even the Provincial Archives. Get rid of it. I made four piles: pitch, keep, library and Salvation Army. After three hours, I was so impressed with myself, I finished filing the last few things away. I even found bank statements from the Canadian Imperial Bank of Commerce for an account that I didn't even know I had. It was such an old account, it showed the balance as a minus, that is, below zero. But, it seemed that on January 1st, the Bank had withdrawn $35 plus tax for an "SDB rental". Hmmm! There was only one thing banks rented, I thought to myself. I set the statement aside, planning to look into it next week.
    If I had a safety deposit box, then I must have a key, no two keys. I vaguely recalled having a safety deposit box when the kids were small. I must have tucked away deeds to my property. I thought hard. Maybe I had forgotten some Canada Savings Bonds in there. Whoo-hoo! Found money! But where were the keys?
    I checked all the special hiding holes I ever had. The safe, the metal box, my old wooden jewellery box, Rob's desk, my first briefcase, my file marked "B" for bank. Nothing. My lime green wallet I kept in the filing cabinet for American money? It only had one piece of fluff in the coin part. No American money and no key.
    O.K. I tried to do the math. We've moved three times in the last ten

years. From R.R. #2 Marchmont to 369 Collins Drive to Horseshoe Valley Road and now to Longford. I remembered we had a whole bunch of keys after the last move. We threw out anything that didn't fit our new house. Damn! That must be what happened. I wondered what new keys would cost. I placed the old bank statement in my daybook, moving it up in importance. I would definitely look into it on Monday.

My oldest son called on Sunday night. "Mom, can we go for lunch tomorrow?" I consulted my daybook.

"Sure, I have to go to the bank anyway."

But, then, I caught on. "Wait a minute. You don't really want me to have lunch, do ya, Jord? How much? How much money do you need?"

Jordie seemed genuinely offended. "I don't need money, Mom. Just thought if you had time, we could have lunch for once."

I felt sheepish. "Wow! My son's taking me for lunch", I said.

"No", Jord admitted. "You're buying."

Rob and I finished our Sunday night dinner and I thought of settling into a fresh 'slasher' novel. But, I thought that since my office was now so ultra clean, I should dust the top of my desk. I should actually dust the fine curved legs of my antique walnut desk. I couldn't remember the last time I had done so.

I got a new damp J-cloth™ from under the kitchen sink. I even thought about taking the camera, to have proof of this proud moment for posterity. I thought to myself, that would be too sick and twisted, even for me. I chuckled.

As I turned to admire my handiwork one last time, I reached to turn out the office light. Something was bugging me. I paused in the doorway, looking at my gleaming, dust-free Louis XVI desk.

Only I knew about my secret shame, that small skinny drawer on the front of my beautiful desk, so well hidden it didn't even have a pull handle. When we moved from Collins Drive, I had so many 'things' to move that my friend, Leila, recognized my frustration. She helped me pack up my office and dining room. What a pal. I laughingly recalled what my father had told me one time about friends. "A friend will help you move. A true friend will help you move the body."

Four years before, when my friend, Leila, helped me pack, she inadvertently discovered the small desk drawer. She pulled it open. I can still see the look on her face. She said simply, "Oh, my!" There were ticket stubs, TTC bus passes, crayons, paper clips, nails, receipts, gum wrappers, Halls™, loose aspirin, a coat check claim ticket, broken pens, chewed off pencils, dog-eared photographs, bath salts, used envelopes, a miniature book of psalms and even a very small green Gumby™. In excellent shape, I might add.

Standing in my west-facing office on Collins Drive, Leila and I decided to dump the whole drawer into an empty shoebox. We labelled it "Sherry's desk drawer". I never had the heart to tell Leila. Well, I have to face it. I never had the heart to tell anyone (until now) what happened after my beautiful old desk got moved into our new house. I dumped the contents of the shoebox back into the desk drawer and shut the drawer quickly, never to see the light of day again.

But the guilt was getting to me. As a responsible adult with an ultra-clean office, it was time. Time to face my demon, the dreaded desk drawer. I was in my 50th year. I had an hour to spare. I am a bright, competent woman, I told myself. Surely, I can handle this. I opened it up quickly before I could change my mind. I had the garbage can nearby and began to sort.

Well, you can guess what happened. Way at the back, stuck to the wood with a used green Lifesaver™ I found not one, but two flat keys strung together with a piece of white string, dirty and sticky, with some kind of black oil on part of the string. Yech! I didn't even want to know what that was. The three-digit number on the one side of each key matched. It was #305. I had my safety deposit box keys for a box I had been paying for, for who knows how long. The secrets of the box would be revealed the next day. I carefully taped the two keys to my bank statement in my 2007 daybook. I couldn't wait.

I met Jord for lunch the next day at the appointed time and place. We talked about work and life, his son Pax and how plans for his good friend Pokey's wedding were well underway. I told Jord it was nice to see Pokey finally settle down. "He plays in a rock band, after all", I mused.

There was something "off" about Jord during our lunch, as I chattered on about my upcoming trip to the south. He didn't quite seem to be himself. He acted like he was listening, but he was distracted.

Never able to quite figure out my grown son of 26 years and being somewhat known for my nosiness, I tried to hang back. Finally, I said, "Jord. What's wrong? Are you okay? Are you sick?"

Jord scoffed at the suggestion. "I'm not sick, Mom. I'm fine, really."

"Then, what is it?" I pressed. "What's going on? What are you thinking?"

He hesitated, clasping his hands together on the table so that they formed a little steeple, a move I'd never seen him make before. "Mom, I need to tell you something." His words came in a rush. "I'm thinking of asking Shannon to marry me."

If my son was looking for an objective opinion, he came to the wrong place. I clapped my hands in excitement. "That's great, Jord. We really like Shannon. I think you've met your match. But, are you sure?"

"Yep, I'm sure. I've thought about it a lot. It's time. I haven't told

Dad. I thought I'd try it out on you first." He had no plan about when to ask Shannon. He only knew it would be soon.

"I'm so happy", I practically gushed. "Are you sure she'll say yes?"

"Yup", Jord said. He was always a man of few words. "She'll say yes."

We parted after our usual cheek kiss goodbye. I was so glad Jord was settling down. I hummed to myself as I headed to the bank. I was even happier knowing I knew what Jord's plan was, before his father (my ex-husband) did.

Obsessive as ever, I had phoned the bank that morning to make sure the keys I had would match the box I had been paying for. After checking their file, they assured me I had the right key.

As a long-standing customer of the bank, the manager met me as I lined up. She took me over to the side counter where the safety deposit box sign-in sheets were kept. I forgot what a big production this would be. The bank manager remarked as I signed my name and she initialled my signature "Looks like it's been almost 10 years since you've accessed this box." I was surprised, but I shouldn't have been. No wonder I had forgotten about it.

We entered the vault and the bank manager inserted her key smoothly, too classy to say anything about the dirty string holding my keys together. She took them from me and tried one. It fit perfectly. The locks tumbled and she slid my box out.

"I'll take you into our private viewing room", she announced.

"Oh, no, that's fine", I protested. "I'm sure there's not much in it, just some papers. Let's just set it here. I won't be long."

She set the box on some metal file boxes beside me, just inside the door. I opened the box. It's long lid now stood straight up. Two manila envelopes were inside. One said "Mom's Will" and the other said "Dad's Will". "Oh, my", I exclaimed.

My father had been dead for 29 years; my mother for 32. Probably, no one will be contesting those wills, I thought to myself.

I took out two Canada Savings Bonds for $100 each in our youngest son's name. They had matured three years ago, not making any more interest. My husband, always thrifty, won't be pleased.

"That's all", I announce to the manager. "No deeds to property. No gold bouillion." I closed the box and handed it back to the manager. "Guess that's it."

Much shorter than I was, the manager put one hand under each end, lifted the box over her head and prepared to slide the box back into its slot. We both heard a rattle.

She handed the box back to me. "Sounds like there's something else."

I took the box back and stood it on its open end on top of the file box. A very small manila envelope, maybe two inches by two inches, fell out. I picked it up and see right away that it's lumpy. The end is sealed. I rip it open and give it a shake. A single ring falls into my hand.

And, suddenly, with the empty envelope in my right hand and a diamond ring glinting in my left hand, I am transported back 40 years to when I am nine years old.

My mother and I are sitting at the kitchen table peeling potatoes. It is daytime and the noon-day sun is streaming into the window making my mother's jet-black hair seem even blacker.

I admire mom's practised hands, deftly peeling potatoes. My job is to wash them in the big glass bowl as she peels. The ring on mom's left hand glints in the sunlight. I stop her in mid peel. Mom allows me to admire her engagement ring. I tilt her hand this way and that, allowing her ring to make little rainbows around the room.

"Will this ring be mine some day, Mommy?" I ask her.

"Oh, probably. See? There are three rings, one for each of my daughters."

"Yeah, but I want the one with the big diamond, Mommy."

My mother laughs and says, "You'll have to negotiate that with your sisters."

"When I have this ring, Mommy, I'll never take it off. I'll wear it every day. I promise."

My mother resumed her peeling. "No, you won't. Some people think they're sentimental, but they're really not. You'll have other jewellery to wear."

I sat listening at the table with my chin resting on my fists. My mother looked pensive for a moment. Then she continued.

"Some day, Sherry Lynn, far off in the future, you'll fall in love and get married. And you'll have children. Pretty good odds, you'll have a boy and a girl. And one day that boy will grow up to be a man. He'll fall in love, but he can't trust his friends. He can only trust his mother. He'll ask you if he should marry the woman he loves. You'll say 'yes'. Because you'll really like her. You'll be so pleased he asked. You'll give him a gift. You'll give him the ring that used to be mine. He'll give it to the woman he loves, when he proposes. And she'll agree to marry your son." She paused. "This ring will bind the families together."

"What does that mean, Mommy?" I asked wide-eyed. "Bind?!"

She put down her potato and knife and took one of my hands with one of hers. Together she forms them into a steeple. My mother makes a gesture around our two steepled hands as if he she was wrapping them together or tying them.

"Bind", she said. "Stuck together. Joined together. See?"

I got it. "Really, Mommy?"

"Really, Sherry Lynn. Now, let's get these potatoes on the stove."

Suddenly, I was back in the bank vault, with the bank manager's hand on my forearm.

"Mrs. Lawson, are you all right?" she asked softly.

The open envelope was still in my right hand. My mother's engagement ring was still in my left. Tears were streaming down my face. I don't' know how long I'd been there. But I knew I'd been given a sign.

I put the ring on my baby finger and the bank manager gave me a really large manila envelope for my paperwork.

I closed my safety deposit box that day and got my last rental payment for the year refunded.

I drove to my son's apartment right away. He was surprised to see me there so soon after lunch. He answered the door after I knocked loudly. We sat down. After I told him the whole story starting with my cleaning out of my desk and ending with my crying in the bank vault.

Then my grown son and I, sitting at his kitchen table, cried together. I knew that a relative my son had never met, my mother, spoke to us today.

It's going to be another exciting year for our family. And, three weeks later, my desk is still clean.

Update February 21, 2007.

Shannon just called crying. Jord proposed today, one week after Valentine's Day. Kids today, so non-traditional. She said "yes".

Late-Breaking News March 9, 2007.

Jord called. They've set the date. It's August 9, 2008. My heart catches in my throat. August 9th is my mother's birthday.

Almost Famous

It seems like my last two jobs have made me a celebrity of sorts. Small town and a slow news week. A deadly combination.

When I was a Justice of the Peace for the Province of Ontario for eight years, I was involved with many court cases, closely watched by the public: drug busts, fish and game cases, environmental protection. All created community interest and, on occasion, members of the public came to sit in court to hear my decisions.

Being the only Native Justice of the Peace in the Central East Region, I already caused a stir wherever I presided: in Toronto at Old City Hall, in bail court in Oshawa, first appearance in Huntsville or Young Offenders Court in Orillia. I raised eyebrows sometimes because of my decisions. I raised even more eyebrows because I carried an eagle feather into court with me. But I digress. The public had begun to notice me.

And then I took a very high profile job as a Casino Rama Director. Imagine, me, a Native woman, with a degree in Anthropology and a certificate in Museum Studies, getting paid to do public relations for a gambling emporium. A big part of my job is giving money to charity: community needs always outnumber the budget. Often my picture is in the paper, smiling with yet another non-profit who can, with my employer's help, feed the hungry, thank their volunteers or train their board. I am also asked to speak to dozens of community groups each year – thousands of people. The citizenry believes they know me. They see me so often, they believe we're friends.

No matter where I go, people stop me to talk, ask me how my family is, call me by name. The very first time I was called to meet my new Vice-President, a lawyer, this became important. It was 8:50 a.m. I was due in her office – upper floor at 9:00 a.m. Lots of time. I hurried across the floor heading to the elevator. Suddenly, an elderly woman stopped me at the 25¢ slots.

"Sherry", she boomed. "How are you? Nice to see you." She shook my hand. "Just a minute. My husband is here somewhere. Earl! Earl! Earl!" An elderly man came around the bank of slot machines. He must have been Earl. I can still recall what he was wearing: blue plaid shirt, jeans, white sneakers, a white belt and white suspenders. I thought that he mustn't be very confident, this Earl - a belt and suspenders! At any rate, it is, indeed, Earl. He comes over to shake my hand, obviously pleased to see me.

"Sherry, how are things? How's your husband. Any grandchildren yet?" I admitted there wasn't a grandchild yet. Eternally well-trained and polite, we chatted for several minutes. I'm running through my mental rolodex trying to figure out how I know Dorothy and Earl. I finally take the opportunity during a break in the conversation to ask this couple how we know each other. Dorothy freely admits that I've never met her and Earl before. "We just feel like we know you. We see your picture in the paper all the time. We've seen you interviewed on the New VR. So, we know you."

I said, "Nice to talk to you. Gotta go."

I headed to the elevator – 1 minute to 9. I blew into my boss's office, breathless, at 9:01. My new Vice-President, casually raised her wristwatch up to her face. "Did we say nine a.m.?"

"I know, I know", I tried to explain. "I walked across the floor and got stopped by Dorothy and Earl."

She looked confused. "Do I know Dorothy and Earl? she asked.

"I don't know Dorothy and Earl." I sat down to tell her my story. It was then I realized that the public believes they own a part of me.

And sometimes it gets tiresome. I even have to arrange where I will hold meetings in the Orillia area – which restaurant will I have lunch in? Because I get interrupted by strangers so often wherever I go.

My friend from the SPCA wanted to take me to lunch to discuss fundraising. How about Maria's™? Nope. Picasso's™? No. Swiss Chalet™? Nah. I always run into too many people I know. "Well", Erin says, a little exasperated, "Where will we go?" I know. She has an idea! "Come to my house for lunch. The paparazzi won't find you there." We laughed. The next week we had a lovely lunch at her home on Tecumseth Street. Outside, on the deck even. I was watching the bushes, though, with one eye out for photographers or reporters. But, amazingly, no one tracked me down that day.

And partway through my tenure at the Casino, I was named the Orillia Business Women's Association "Woman of the Year" in 2004. That's when things started to get a little weird.

My friend, Brenda, and I go to lawn sales every Saturday morning three seasons of the year. Wherever we go, people know me. They talk to me like we're old friends. They ask me about my family, my vacation plans, my sleeping patterns. Strangers know way too much about me. One time, I found a garage sale dresser that was too big for my car. I said I'd return for it later, with the truck. Did she need my name and phone number? "Oh, no", she chirped. "You're Sherry Lawson ." Brenda rolled her eyes. On the way to the car, she says, "If one more person says 'Woman of the Year', I'm going to punch their lights out!" Brenda's too polite and too good a Catholic to actually punch anyone out. Good thing.

Recently, Brenda and I were second-handing. I took my few purchases to the check out. The saleslady practically gushed. "Sherry, how are you?" She was totally ignoring Brenda, probably would have pushed Brenda aside if necessary. "You know", my new friend rattled on. "I've kept a scrapbook on you. Every time you're in the paper, I cut it out and date it. You're famous, you know." I believe she was reaching under the counter to show me the scrapbook of my life, but I never got to see it. Brenda dragged me out of there, lecturing me all the way to the car, something about stalkers. Spooky!

In the late summer of 2005, I was travelling with my husband to Sault Ste. Marie. Now, there aren't a lot of fuel, snack or washroom stops on the way. Everyone stops in Blind River at Tim Horton's™. Clean washrooms, good service. So I'm innocently washing my hands in the public bathroom like my mother, the nurse, always taught me. A young woman is beside me at the other sink doing the same thing. She kept looking at me out of the corner of her eye, trying to get a good look, but trying not to let on. As I dried my hands, I finally looked at this stranger directly and said, "Excuse me, do I know you?" even though this time I knew I didn't.

"No", she responded. "But, aren't you Sherry Lawson, Business Woman of the Year?"

I must have had a strange look on my face. "Who are you?"

"Oh, you don't know me", she said. "My mother was at the Orillia Business Women's Dinner the night you won. She sent me your picture out of the paper."

"How nice", I said, backing out of the bathroom and sprinting to the car.

A full year later, in the summer of 2006, I was, again, out with my best friend Brenda. We stopped at the closest Tim Horton's™ (in Atherley) to get me a cold drink and Brenda a ½ coffee, ½ hot chocolate, mid morning pick-me-up, as is our Saturday custom.

I got up to the drive-through window and someone I didn't recognize, wearing a Tim Horton's™ hat, leaned out and said, "Hey, aren't you Sherry

Lawson, Business Woman of the Year?" I had to admit I was.

"Hey, girls. It's the Business Woman of the Year", she announced to her work mates. They started to applaud. She leaned out of the window as I thanked her. "Your drink is free, but hers (she said and pointed at Brenda) is $1.57."

I tossed her a toonie, told her to keep the change and peeled out of there before Brenda could get out and punch her lights out. I believe Brenda's door was already open.

The year 2005 turns into 2006 and then into 2007. I figure my front-page photo is just a distant memory. Apparently, not in Orillia.

In April 2007, I purchased a new Subaru™ . I have had personalized plates for more than 10 years on other cars. This time I thought I'd be radical. With a new vehicle and new licence plates I can be totally anonymous. I thought to myself, no one will know me.

I picked up my new vehicle and had just enough time to drop off a box of used household items to the "Green Again" second-hand store in downtown Orillia. I parked behind the old Zellers™ in downtown Orillia and used my shiny new key fob to lock all the doors. Pleased with myself, I was actually whistling as I headed to the stairs and carried my little box. An elderly woman with a cane was entering at the same time. She held the door open for me. Smiling, she said "New car, eh? And I see you got new plates, too."

I must have looked stunned. "Do I know you, Madame?"

"Oh no, dear. But everyone knows you." She toddled off down the hallway. "Nice Subaru™!"

So much for being incognito.

Because so many members of the public know me, when I am on vacation, I leave town. Otherwise, I'm always working. Better yet, I leave the country.

Several months ago, my husband and I took off for the week-end, last minute to travel to New York. I could spend some quality time with my spouse, have a nice meal, slip in some shopping, all in a place where no one would know me. Paradise...

I was in gigantic change room with about 15 outfits to try on. My husband, Rob, sat in the car waiting for me. It's not that much fun for him to shop with me, or so he says.

Things are going along swimmingly. The first four outfits out of five are looking good. The store was busy. I hear a light tapping on the wall. I figure it's someone looking for their mother, sister, friend, in an adjoining change room. In my underwear, I ignore it and continue trying on clothes. The tapping becomes more insistent and turns into knocking on the wall of my change room.

My train of thought is totally interrupted and I say aloud to the wall,

"Excuse me, are you knocking for me?"

A middle-aged disembodied voice floated over the change room wall divider. "Yes, aren't you Sherry Lawson, Business Woman of the Year?"

"Yes! Who the hell are you?" I answer quite sharply.

"Oh, you don't know me", says the voice I don't recognize. "I live in Washago and I always wanted to meet you."

That's it. I put on my clothes and leave the change room in a big mess. I practically run out of the store to the car. Rob is non-plussed as I tell him this latest story. In fact, he thinks it's hilarious.

There I am on vacation in another country and someone knows me. Or they think they do. Frightening!

Sometimes I dream of my younger days when I lived my life in relative obscurity. Will I ever just be another anonymous citizen? Probably not. My husband tells me that a part of me likes being "almost famous." If we each only get 15 minutes of fame, I wonder when the timekeeper's watch stopped ticking for me.

Sherry Lawson, Business Woman of The Year (2004) and her friend Brenda.

Sherry working in Orillia's Courthouse as Justice of the Peace, 1998

After-Word

It occurs to me that since I have started to write down my stories, I am missing a crucial part of my life as a storyteller - an audience.

The beauty of telling a story is having instant audience reaction: laughter, tears, applause, the wave of a hand and even the occasional "Go on with ya!" I miss that.

I encourage you to contact me if you feel so inclined. E-mail me at mailto:maangdodem@hotmail.com. Tell me if my stories have offered a glimpse, if not into my own life, then into that of my family.

Or, perhaps, you have been reminded of something. And now you feel obliged to put pen to paper yourself.

I am but a simple storyteller.

Sherry Lawson
August 2007

Sherry's Father in the army

Sherry's Mother as a young woman

Sherry's mother as a young girl (8)

Sherry's childhood home

ove: Sherry and Rob visit the Grand Ole Opry

The walkway at the HRC, where Sherry's mother worked for many years

eiling Weirs plaque,
er/chief in head-dress

View of Geneva Park Bay

An excerpt from Sherry's next book

"My father's gravestone is nearby. Plain. Paid for by the Federal Department of Veteran's Affairs. Just the way Dad wanted it. I've put a beautiful dreamcatcher and willow basket in the tree over his grave. The woman who sold it to me for $5 at a lawn sale said it was made in Arizona by a "real Indian". She brought it back herself. I don't know if that's a true story, but the handiwork is exquisite."